JUMBLE® CHAMPION

The Undisputed King of Puzzles!

Henri Arnold,
Bob Lee,
David L. Hoyt
and Jeff Knurek

TRIUMPH
BOOKS

For further information, contact:
Triumph Books LLC
814 North Franklin Street
Chicago, Illinois 60610
Phone: (312) 337-0747
www.triumphbooks.com

Printed in U.S.A.

ISBN: 978-1-62937-870-1

Design by Sue Knopf

CONTENTS

JUMBLE®

CHAMPION

Classic Puzzles

JUMBLE®

Unscramble these four Jumbles, one letter to each square, to form four ordinary words.

CUVOH

IMODI

ENZARB

GOTTOR

Who invited HIM?

HOW DID THE TRUMPET PLAYER MANAGE TO GET INTO THAT EXCLUSIVE PARTY?

Now arrange the circled letters to form the surprise answer, as suggested by the above cartoon.

Print answer here HE " ⬡⬡⬡⬡⬡⬡ " IN

JUMBLE®

Unscramble these four Jumbles, one letter to each square, to form four ordinary words.

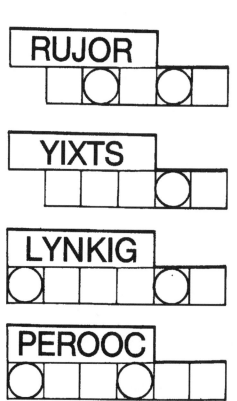

RUJOR

YIXTS

LYNKIG

PEROOC

WHAT YOU'RE LIKELY TO TAKE WHEN YOU'RE INVITED TO DINNER BY WITCHES.

Now arrange the circled letters to form the surprise answer, as suggested by the above cartoon.

Print answer here

JUMBLE®

Unscramble these four Jumbles, one letter to each square, to form four ordinary words.

ETTIL

GORRI

MELTIG

NIWWON

WHAT HAPPENED TO THE BELL THAT FELL INTO THE WATER?

Now arrange the circled letters to form the surprise answer, as suggested by the above cartoon.

Print answer here   IT WAS " ⬡⬡⬡⬡⬡⬡⬡⬡ " ⬡⬡⬡

4

JUMBLE®

Unscramble these four Jumbles, one letter
to each square, to form four ordinary words.

LASIE

VAINE

DUBUSE

TUPIRD

I love game

WHY IS VENISON
SO EXPENSIVE?

Now arrange the circled letters
to form the surprise answer, as
suggested by the above cartoon.

Print answer here ◯◯' ◯ "◯◯◯◯◯"

JUMBLE®

Unscramble these four Jumbles, one letter to each square, to form four ordinary words.

KLANB

ARCTT

ADUMAR

MUGLEE

WHAT HAPPENED TO THE PLASTIC SURGEON WHO WAS WORKING IN AN OVERHEATED OPERATING ROOM?

Now arrange the circled letters to form the surprise answer, as suggested by the above cartoon.

Print answer here HE ⬡⬡⬡⬡⬡⬡⬡

JUMBLE®

Unscramble these four Jumbles, one letter to each square, to form four ordinary words.

ORDOB

HIEWL

YORPOL

DIRAUM

DIRTY SWABS!

SQUAWK!

WHAT'S A PARROT?

Now arrange the circled letters to form the surprise answer, as suggested by the above cartoon.

Print answer here   A

7

JUMBLE®

Unscramble these four Jumbles, one letter
to each square, to form four ordinary words.

NOOZE

MAALL

DIPTUN

YAQUES

LOVES SKIN
DIVING.

Now arrange the circled letters
to form the surprise answer, as
suggested by the above cartoon.

Print answer here A

JUMBLE®

Unscramble these four Jumbles, one letter
to each square, to form four ordinary words.

SHOWE

HECKE

DRIZAL

LIZZES

WHAT HIS RICH
UNCLE WHO WAS A
FAMOUS ARTIST KNEW
HOW TO DRAW BEST.

Now arrange the circled letters
to form the surprise answer, as
suggested by the above cartoon.

Print answer here

JUMBLE®

Unscramble these four Jumbles, one letter to each square, to form four ordinary words.

DELAL
◯◯☐◯☐

KUSYD
☐☐◯☐☐

COLLEA
◯☐◯☐☐◯

SUMPAC
☐◯◯☐☐◯

HOW THE WEIGHING MACHINE TYCOON STARTED IN BUSINESS.

Now arrange the circled letters to form the surprise answer, as suggested by the above cartoon.

Print answer here ON A ◯◯◯◯◯ ◯◯◯◯◯

JUMBLE®

Unscramble these four Jumbles, one letter
to each square, to form four ordinary words.

RYKUM

BOSEE

LURCUN

STIPTY

HOW TO GET YOUR
WIFE TO BAKE THOSE
DELICIOUS ROLLS.

Now arrange the circled letters
to form the surprise answer, as
suggested by the above cartoon.

Print answer here ⬡⬡⬡⬡⬡⬡ HER ⬡⬡

JUMBLE®

Unscramble these four Jumbles, one letter
to each square, to form four ordinary words.

NIRED

YUCIJ

REEPAM

NIFTIE

WHAT THE
FRIGHTENED
ROCK WAS.

Now arrange the circled letters
to form the surprise answer, as
suggested by the above cartoon.

Print answer here " ◯◯◯◯◯◯◯◯◯◯ "

JUMBLE®

Unscramble these four Jumbles, one letter
to each square, to form four ordinary words.

ACTUD

ESSOU

FRYTAC

TYKONT

BANG!

WHAT TO DO
WHEN A PLUG
DOESN'T FIT.

Now arrange the circled letters
to form the surprise answer, as
suggested by the above cartoon.

Print answer here " ⬡◯◯◯◯◯◯ "

JUMBLE®

Unscramble these four Jumbles, one letter to each square, to form four ordinary words.

ILLAC

IGNAT

TYDWAR

CUNNEA

WHAT THEY WERE DOING ON THAT TELEVISED BALLET.

Now arrange the circled letters to form the surprise answer, as suggested by the above cartoon.

Print answer here ⬡⬡⬡⬡⬡⬡⬡ ON ⬡⬡⬡

Unscramble these four Jumbles, one letter
to each square, to form four ordinary words.

CINEE

INVEX

BLIRME

INBENG

Sorry, Ronald—you're
not my type

HOW THE VAMPIRE
LOVED.

Now arrange the circled letters
to form the surprise answer, as
suggested by the above cartoon.

Print answer here ◯◯ " ◯◯◯◯ "

JUMBLE®

Unscramble these four Jumbles, one letter to each square, to form four ordinary words.

FRASC

WELJE

DRAWZI

KEBTUC

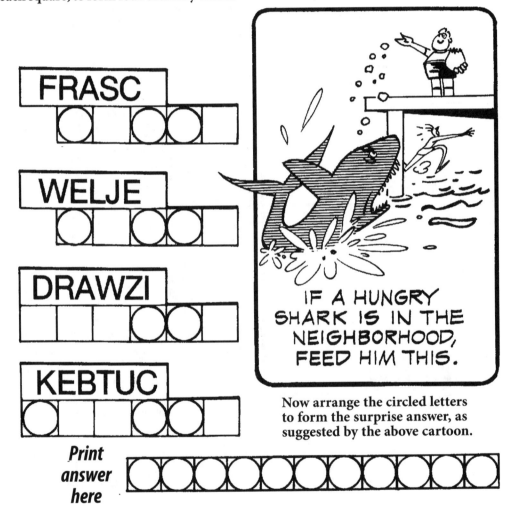

IF A HUNGRY
SHARK IS IN THE
NEIGHBORHOOD,
FEED HIM THIS.

Now arrange the circled letters to form the surprise answer, as suggested by the above cartoon.

Print answer here

JUMBLE®

Unscramble these four Jumbles, one letter
to each square, to form four ordinary words.

ELROD
◻◻◯◻◻

NARFC
◻◻◯◯◻

LAYREY
◯◻◻◻◻◯

AUSANE
◯◻◯◯◻◻

Can't take too many
precautions

WHAT THE
UMBRELLA MERCHANT
WAS SAVING HIS
MONEY FOR.

Now arrange the circled letters
to form the surprise answer, as
suggested by the above cartoon.

Print answer here A ◯◯◯◯◯◯ ◯◯◯

JUMBLE®

Unscramble these four Jumbles, one letter
to each square, to form four ordinary words.

PUBYM

CRAID

TALBOC

DOINIE

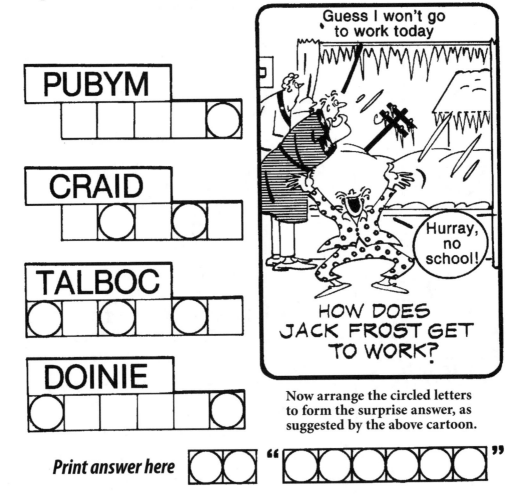

Guess I won't go
to work today

Hurray,
no
school!

HOW DOES
JACK FROST GET
TO WORK?

Now arrange the circled letters
to form the surprise answer, as
suggested by the above cartoon.

Print answer here "   "

JUMBLE®

Unscramble these four Jumbles, one letter
to each square, to form four ordinary words.

WARLD

HACCO

REHAWL

SKUTEM

THE SHIP DOCKED
NEAR THE BARBERSHOP
BECAUSE THEY ALL
NEEDED THIS.

Now arrange the circled letters
to form the surprise answer, as
suggested by the above cartoon.

Print answer here " ⬡⬡⬡⬡⬡ " ⬡⬡⬡⬡

JUMBLE®

Unscramble these four Jumbles, one letter
to each square, to form four ordinary words.

THILG

KUSHY

CEEDOD

NICRIO

THE TURKEY CROSSED
THE ROAD TO
PROVE THIS.

Now arrange the circled letters
to form the surprise answer, as
suggested by the above cartoon.

*Print
answer
here* ◯◯ WASN'T " ◯◯◯◯◯◯◯ "

JUMBLE®

Unscramble these four Jumbles, one letter
to each square, to form four ordinary words.

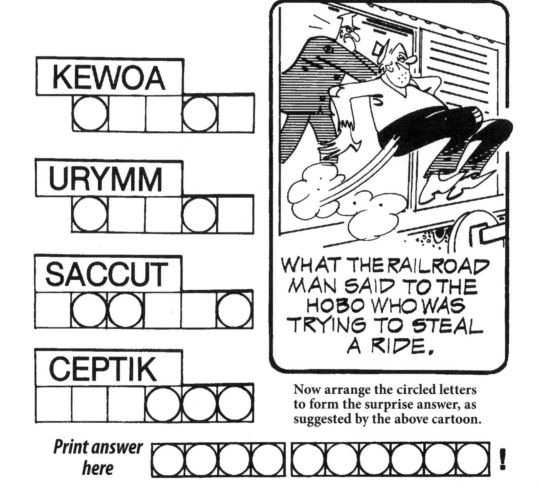

KEWOA

URYMM

SACCUT

CEPTIK

WHAT THE RAILROAD
MAN SAID TO THE
HOBO WHO WAS
TRYING TO STEAL
A RIDE.

Now arrange the circled letters
to form the surprise answer, as
suggested by the above cartoon.

*Print answer
here* ◯◯◯◯ ◯◯◯◯◯◯ !

JUMBLE®

Unscramble these four Jumbles, one letter to each square, to form four ordinary words.

CRYPTOGRAPHY
ROOM

WHAT THE SECRET AGENT WAS COMPLAINING OF.

DUTOO

FLECT

EDGERD

BORRAH

Now arrange the circled letters to form the surprise answer, as suggested by the above cartoon.

Print answer here   A " ◯◯◯◯ " IN THE ◯◯◯◯

JUMBLE®

Unscramble these four Jumbles, one letter to each square, to form four ordinary words.

SOONE

YOWND

BLUBEA

YARNTT

LOONY BIN

WHY THEY HAD TO PUT THE VAMPIRE AWAY.

Now arrange the circled letters to form the surprise answer, as suggested by the above cartoon.

Print answer here HE ◯◯◯◯ ◯◯◯◯

JUMBLE®

Unscramble these four Jumbles, one letter
to each square, to form four ordinary words.

MOBOL

CEENF

UNSLIM

QUIDIL

WHAT THE DOCTOR
SAID WHEN THE
PATIENT COMPLAINED
OF RINGING IN
HIS EARS.

Now arrange the circled letters
to form the surprise answer, as
suggested by the above cartoon.

*Print
answer
here* YOU'RE ⬡⬡⬡⬡⬡ AS A ⬡⬡⬡⬡

JUMBLE®

Unscramble these four Jumbles, one letter
to each square, to form four ordinary words.

DITIO

SUDOE

JEDGAG

BRUMEN

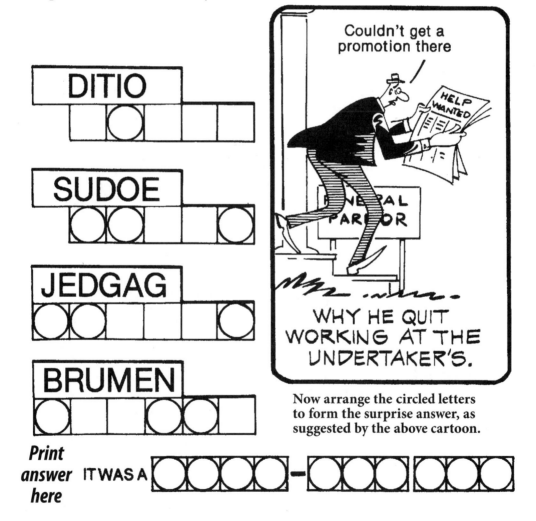

Couldn't get a
promotion there

FUNERAL PARLOR

HELP WANTED

WHY HE QUIT
WORKING AT THE
UNDERTAKER'S.

Now arrange the circled letters
to form the surprise answer, as
suggested by the above cartoon.

**Print
answer
here** IT WAS A ⬭⬭⬭⬭-⬭⬭⬭ ⬭⬭⬭

JUMBLE®

Unscramble these four Jumbles, one letter to each square, to form four ordinary words.

YOLID

BOVAR

SCYTIK

EMFONT

WHEN A VANDAL MADE A HOLE IN THE FENCE AT THE NUDIST CAMP, THE COPS SAID THEY'D DO THIS.

Now arrange the circled letters to form the surprise answer, as suggested by the above cartoon.

Print answer here ⬡⬡⬡⬡ ⬡⬡⬡⬡ IT

JUMBLE®

CHAMPION

Daily Puzzles

JUMBLE®

**Unscramble these four Jumbles, one letter
to each square, to form four ordinary words.**

PRAID

LAWRC

EXCOBI

NYLARX

WHAT HE GOT WHEN
HE READ THE STORY
ABOUT THOSE
BODY SNATCHERS.

Now arrange the circled letters
to form the surprise answer, as
suggested by the above cartoon.

**Print
answer
here**

JUMBLE®

Unscramble these four Jumbles, one letter
to each square, to form four ordinary words.

THOOP

BASUQ

NAEVLE

MUGNIP

WHAT "HMS
PINAFORE" COULD
UNDOUBTEDLY BE.

Now arrange the circled letters
to form the surprise answer, as
suggested by the above cartoon.

Print answer
here "⬡⬡⬡⬡ FOR ⬡⬡⬡⬡"

29

JUMBLE®

Unscramble these four Jumbles, one letter to each square, to form four ordinary words.

NELEK

BROEP

TERVOX

CAYGLE

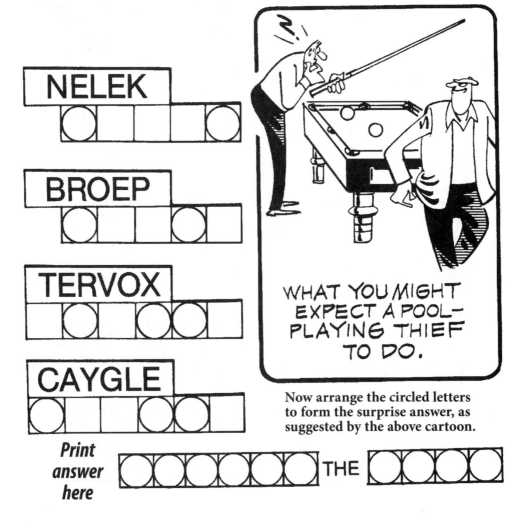

WHAT YOU MIGHT EXPECT A POOL-PLAYING THIEF TO DO.

Now arrange the circled letters to form the surprise answer, as suggested by the above cartoon.

Print answer here

◯◯◯◯◯◯◯ THE ◯◯◯◯

JUMBLE®

Unscramble these four Jumbles, one letter
to each square, to form four ordinary words.

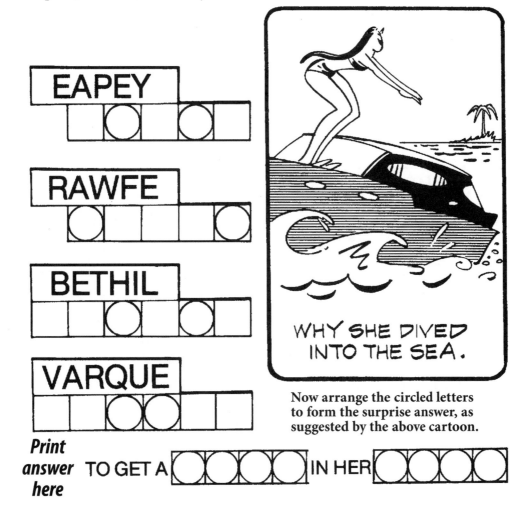

EAPEY

RAWFE

BETHIL

VARQUE

WHY SHE DIVED
INTO THE SEA.

Now arrange the circled letters
to form the surprise answer, as
suggested by the above cartoon.

**Print
answer
here**   TO GET A ⬡⬡⬡⬡ IN HER ⬡⬡⬡⬡

JUMBLE®

Unscramble these four Jumbles, one letter to each square, to form four ordinary words.

DAJED

KEVOE

BARNEY

CLITIE

ONE CAT TOLD THE OTHER TO BE CAREFUL LEST HE DO THIS.

Now arrange the circled letters to form the surprise answer, as suggested by the above cartoon.

Print answer here ◯◯◯ UP IN THAT ◯◯◯◯◯◯

32

JUMBLE®

Unscramble these four Jumbles, one letter
to each square, to form four ordinary words.

NAYLK

BITOR

TESACK

PLAACA

WHAT CHIROPRACTORS
CAN EXPECT A
LOT OF.

Now arrange the circled letters
to form the surprise answer, as
suggested by the above cartoon.

Print answer here

JUMBLE®

Unscramble these four Jumbles, one letter to each square, to form four ordinary words.

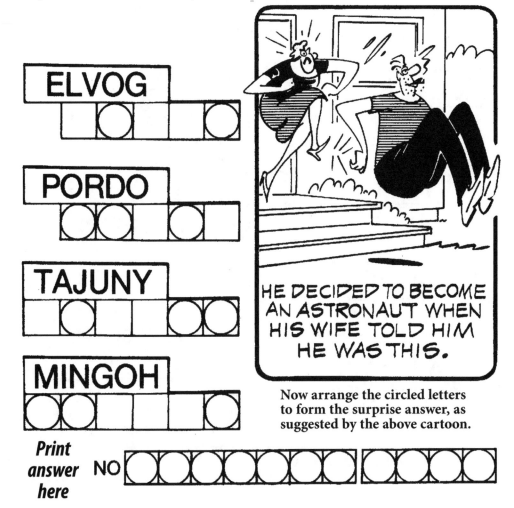

ELVOG

PORDO

TAJUNY

MINGOH

HE DECIDED TO BECOME AN ASTRONAUT WHEN HIS WIFE TOLD HIM HE WAS THIS.

Now arrange the circled letters to form the surprise answer, as suggested by the above cartoon.

Print answer here

NO

JUMBLE®

Unscramble these four Jumbles, one letter
to each square, to form four ordinary words.

PINYP

SABIN

TOINNE

DRAFIT

HEALTH CENTER

IF YOU WANT TO
START LOSING WEIGHT,
YOU CAN GET
INITIATED FROM THIS.

Now arrange the circled letters
to form the surprise answer, as
suggested by the above cartoon.

Print answer
here   A "⬡⬡⬡⬡⬡⬡⬡⬡⬡"

JUMBLE®

Unscramble these four Jumbles, one letter
to each square, to form four ordinary words.

CHARP

NACYF

MENIER

RASTUX

WHERE DO
ALL THE
FLEAS GO
IN WINTER?

Now arrange the circled letters
to form the surprise answer, as
suggested by the above cartoon.

Print answer here "⬡⬡⬡⬡⬡⬡ ⬡⬡"

JUMBLE®

Unscramble these four Jumbles, one letter
to each square, to form four ordinary words.

MIRGE

INAFT

LOMOGY

RUGEDD

THE COFFEE TYCOON
DECIDED TO RETIRE
BECAUSE HE COULDN'T
STAND THIS.

Now arrange the circled letters
to form the surprise answer, as
suggested by the above cartoon.

**Print
answer
here**

THE "⬡⬡⬡⬡⬡ ⬡⬡⬡⬡⬡"

JUMBLE®

Unscramble these four Jumbles, one letter to each square, to form four ordinary words.

TUINY

SITOF

PEAQUO

CLIPSE

WHAT A WISE—
CRACKER DOES.

Now arrange the circled letters to form the surprise answer, as suggested by the above cartoon.

Print answer here

JUMBLE®

Unscramble these four Jumbles, one letter
to each square, to form four ordinary words.

THYIC

MOCTE

FACSIO

PORTSY

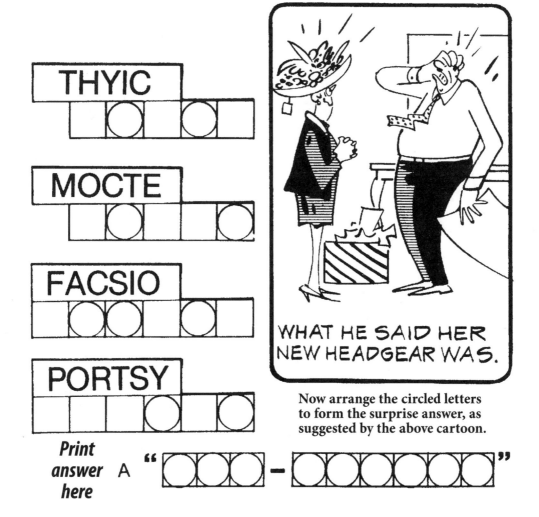

WHAT HE SAID HER
NEW HEADGEAR WAS.

Now arrange the circled letters
to form the surprise answer, as
suggested by the above cartoon.

Print
answer   A "◯◯◯ – ◯◯◯◯◯◯"
here

39

JUMBLE®

Unscramble these four Jumbles, one letter to each square, to form four ordinary words.

PROUG

WOPOH

DORNEV

LARULP

THE TUBA PLAYER LIKED HIS WORK BECAUSE HE WAS THIS.

Now arrange the circled letters to form the surprise answer, as suggested by the above cartoon.

Print answer here ⬡⬡⬡⬡⬡⬡⬡ ⬡⬡ IN IT

JUMBLE®

Unscramble these four Jumbles, one letter
to each square, to form four ordinary words.

EPSIO

TAPAD

BROMEY

FLEEDI

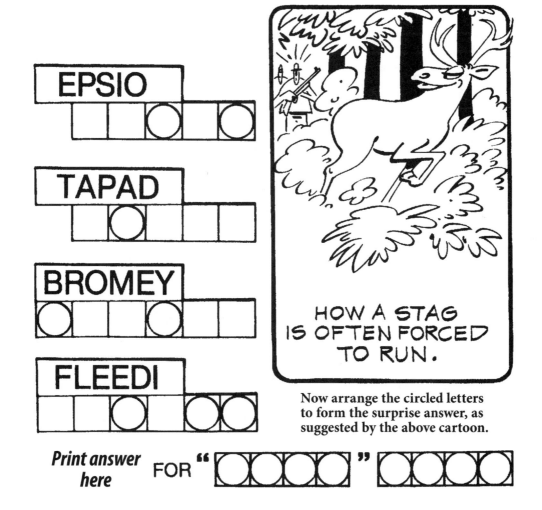

HOW A STAG
IS OFTEN FORCED
TO RUN.

Now arrange the circled letters
to form the surprise answer, as
suggested by the above cartoon.

**Print answer
here** FOR " ◯◯◯◯ " ◯◯◯◯

JUMBLE®

Unscramble these four Jumbles, one letter
to each square, to form four ordinary words.

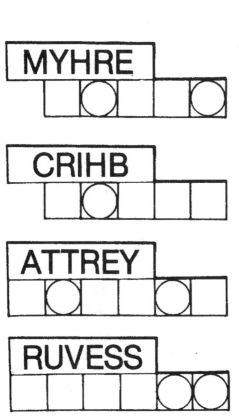

MYHRE

CRIHB

ATTREY

RUVESS

She's going
to be sorry

SHE HAS MANY
A SUITOR BUT
NONE DO THIS.

Now arrange the circled letters
to form the surprise answer, as
suggested by the above cartoon.

Print answer here

JUMBLE®

Unscramble these four Jumbles, one letter
to each square, to form four ordinary words.

GUNST

WYDDO

RIVFEY

TRYSOF

WHAT PEOPLE
WHO GROWL
ALL DAY OFTEN
FEEL AT NIGHT.

Now arrange the circled letters
to form the surprise answer, as
suggested by the above cartoon.

Print answer here ◯◯◯ – ◯◯◯◯◯

JUMBLE®

Unscramble these four Jumbles, one letter
to each square, to form four ordinary words.

TUXEL

GYTIN

ROAMON

PLECOI

HOW SOCIETY
GIRLS START IN.

Now arrange the circled letters
to form the surprise answer, as
suggested by the above cartoon.

*Print answer
here* BY ◯◯◯◯◯◯ " ◯◯◯ "

JUMBLE®

Unscramble these four Jumbles, one letter
to each square, to form four ordinary words.

LOBAT

BAFLE

HOGUNE

GODINI

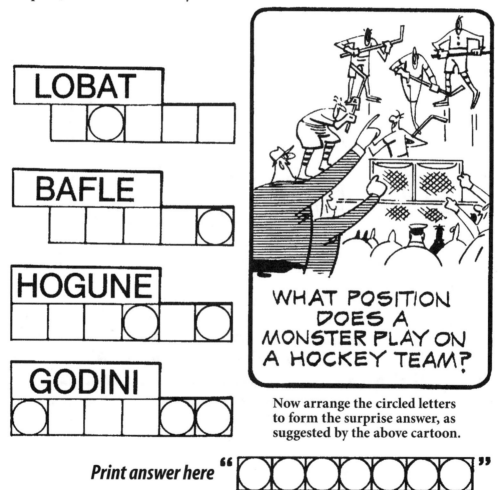

WHAT POSITION
DOES A
MONSTER PLAY ON
A HOCKEY TEAM?

Now arrange the circled letters
to form the surprise answer, as
suggested by the above cartoon.

Print answer here "⟨⟩⟨⟩⟨⟩⟨⟩⟨⟩⟨⟩⟨⟩"

JUMBLE®

Unscramble these four Jumbles, one letter to each square, to form four ordinary words.

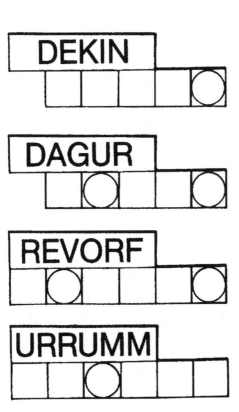

DEKIN

DAGUR

REVORF

URRUMM

Shape up or ship out!

THIS IS A
STERN NECESSITY
ON A BOAT.

Now arrange the circled letters to form the surprise answer, as suggested by the above cartoon.

Print answer here A

JUMBLE®

Unscramble these four Jumbles, one letter
to each square, to form four ordinary words.

DUJEG

HUTEC

INVOIL

TOPITE

And what kind of
work do you do?

WHAT A SECRET
AGENT HAS TO KNOW
HOW TO DO IN ORDER
TO HOLD HIS JOB.

Now arrange the circled letters
to form the surprise answer, as
suggested by the above cartoon.

**Print
answer
here**

◯◯◯◯ HIS ◯◯◯◯◯◯

JUMBLE®

Unscramble these four Jumbles, one letter
to each square, to form four ordinary words.

MYTHE

BECAL

ERTOPY

TANCAV

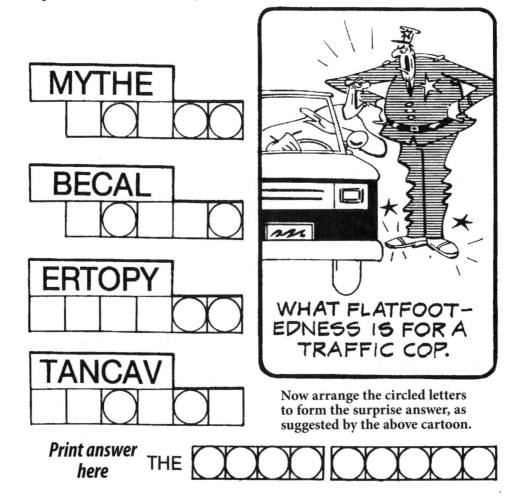

WHAT FLATFOOT-
EDNESS IS FOR A
TRAFFIC COP.

Now arrange the circled letters
to form the surprise answer, as
suggested by the above cartoon.

Print answer here THE ⬡⬡⬡⬡⬡ ⬡⬡⬡⬡⬡⬡

48

JUMBLE®

Unscramble these four Jumbles, one letter
to each square, to form four ordinary words.

TURBS

PEINT

MOODDE

DOPAME

Someday it'll be
worth millions!

Really?

FOR
SALE

WHAT A FALL
GUY IS.

Now arrange the circled letters
to form the surprise answer, as
suggested by the above cartoon.

Print
answer A ⬡⬡⬡⬡ THAT'S A ⬡⬡⬡⬡
here

JUMBLE®

Unscramble these four Jumbles, one letter
to each square, to form four ordinary words.

MYKOS

SCERS

RAFIAS

SIEMUS

THAT DON JUAN
THINKS IT'S NEVER
AMISS TO DO THIS.

Now arrange the circled letters
to form the surprise answer, as
suggested by the above cartoon.

Print answer here

JUMBLE®

Unscramble these four Jumbles, one letter
to each square, to form four ordinary words.

RYRUH

RIBBE

LOMBAG

HURSTH

No hurry, driver

BEER 5¢

THOSE DAYS WERE
LESS HUSTLE
AND MORE THIS.

Now arrange the circled letters
to form the surprise answer, as
suggested by the above cartoon.

Print answer here

JUMBLE®

Unscramble these four Jumbles, one letter
to each square, to form four ordinary words.

MOACE

UNDOB

CRANDI

STEFFO

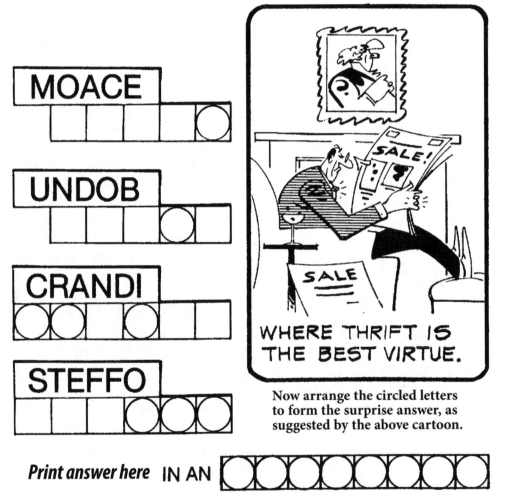

WHERE THRIFT IS
THE BEST VIRTUE.

Now arrange the circled letters
to form the surprise answer, as
suggested by the above cartoon.

Print answer here IN AN ☐☐☐☐☐☐☐☐

JUMBLE

Unscramble these four Jumbles, one letter to each square, to form four ordinary words.

CINEW

CIWET

NORLEG

MIFYAN

How am I supposed to meet my friends when I'm doing this? The grass isn't even that long.

Less talking, more walking.

HIS SON COMPLAINED ABOUT HAVING TO CUT THE GRASS. HE WISHED HE'D STOP HIS ----

Now arrange the circled letters to form the surprise answer, as suggested by the above cartoon.

Print answer here " ◯◯◯ - ◯◯◯◯ "

JUMBLE®

Unscramble these four Jumbles, one letter
to each square, to form four ordinary words.

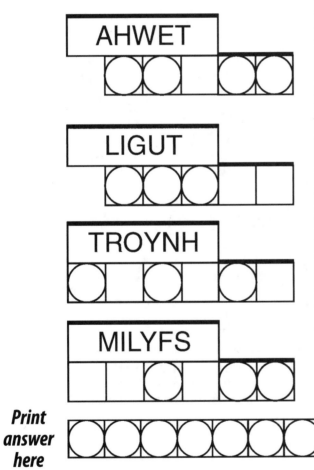

AHWET

LIGUT

TROYNH

MILYFS

Penn & Teller
OPENING ACT AUDITIONS

MIMES DON'T SPEAK DURING
A PERFORMANCE...
OF COURSE THAT GOES ----

Now arrange the circled letters
to form the surprise answer, as
suggested by the above cartoon.

Print
answer
here

JUMBLE®

Unscramble these four Jumbles, one letter
to each square, to form four ordinary words.

PAHYP

GOCIL

GAMEDA

LORHEL

THE BOTTLES OF
SODA WERE ON SALE
FOR A ----

Now arrange the circled letters
to form the surprise answer, as
suggested by the above cartoon.

Print
answer
here

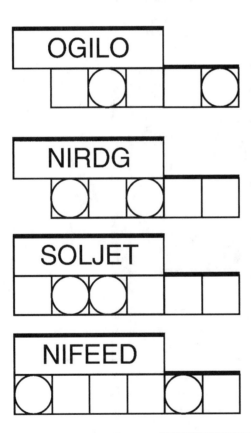

JUMBLE®

Unscramble these four Jumbles, one letter
to each square, to form four ordinary words.

OGILO

NIRDG

SOLJET

NIFEED

SHE WASN'T SURE THE NEW
BILLBOARD WOULD WORK,
BUT SALES INCREASED,
WHICH WAS A ----

Now arrange the circled letters
to form the surprise answer, as
suggested by the above cartoon.

*Print answer
here*

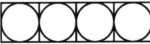

Unscramble these four Jumbles, one letter to each square, to form four ordinary words.

SLACS

RNIKD

TOMSED

NRCEWH

Why did I stay in?

I think a royal flush will win the pot. Am I right?

We didn't stand a chance.

HAVING BEEN DEALT A ROYAL FLUSH, SHE WON ----

Now arrange the circled letters to form the surprise answer, as suggested by the above cartoon.

Print answer here

JUMBLE®

Unscramble these four Jumbles, one letter to each square, to form four ordinary words.

XLIEE

CERKW

GAMMUN

ROYREN

We're having a fireworks display for them.

I've created a vase to celebrate the new dynasty!

The vases are beautiful.

AFTER THE COLLAPSE OF THE YUAN DYNASTY, MANY IN CHINA WERE ----

Now arrange the circled letters to form the surprise answer, as suggested by the above cartoon.

Print answer here " ◯◯◯◯◯◯◯ - ◯◯◯◯ "

JUMBLE®

Unscramble these four Jumbles, one letter to each square, to form four ordinary words.

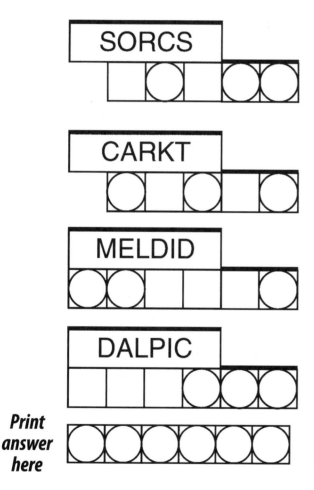

SORCS

CARKT

MELDID

DALPIC

Mac! The 1,000 goldfish you ordered for the show just arrived.

MAGIC

Nice try, Bill! Not on April Fools' Day!

Mac King

IT WAS HARD TO PULL A PRANK ON THE MAGICIAN BECAUSE HE NEVER ---

Now arrange the circled letters to form the surprise answer, as suggested by the above cartoon.

Print answer here

JUMBLE®

Unscramble these four Jumbles, one letter
to each square, to form four ordinary words.

TIHHC

SOLFS

PRYTAN

WAMEDO

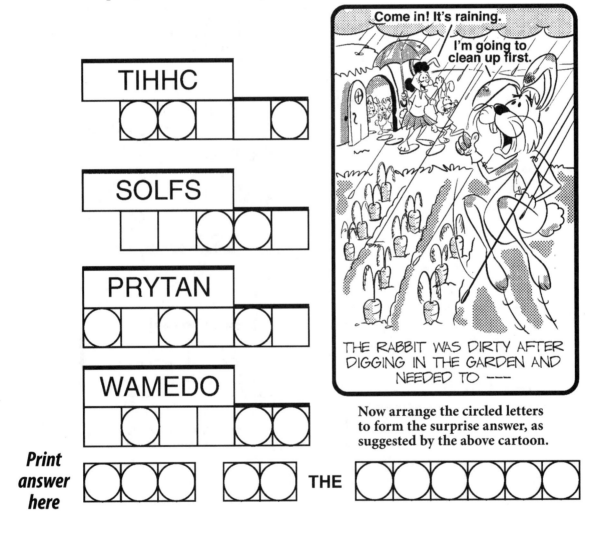

Come in! It's raining.

I'm going to
clean up first.

THE RABBIT WAS DIRTY AFTER
DIGGING IN THE GARDEN AND
NEEDED TO ----

Now arrange the circled letters
to form the surprise answer, as
suggested by the above cartoon.

Print answer here

◯◯◯ ◯◯ THE ◯◯◯◯◯◯

JUMBLE

Unscramble these four Jumbles, one letter
to each square, to form four ordinary words.

WAARE

SREDS

DONLUF

GUFNIM

Trust me,
those are
NOT cows!

This is
horrible!

AFTER REALIZING THAT THEY'D
RECEIVED ONLY BULLS, THE
NEW DAIRY FARM WAS AN ----

Now arrange the circled letters
to form the surprise answer, as
suggested by the above cartoon.

Print
answer
here

" ◯◯◯◯◯ " ◯◯◯◯◯◯◯◯

JUMBLE®

Unscramble these four Jumbles, one letter
to each square, to form four ordinary words.

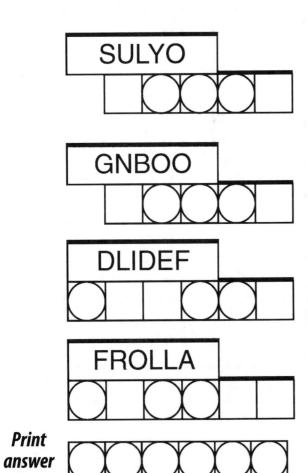

SULYO

GNBOO

DLIDEF

FROLLA

THE 18-HOLE COURSE WOULD
BE LAID OUT IN A CIRCLE,
MAKING IT PERFECT FOR ----

Now arrange the circled letters
to form the surprise answer, as
suggested by the above cartoon.

Print
answer
here

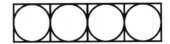

JUMBLE®

Unscramble these four Jumbles, one letter
to each square, to form four ordinary words.

TAYFT

CIGIN

DUSOTI

CONEBU

I can't believe we didn't have more customers.

I guess we chose the wrong location.

IF THE SHOE FITS

STORE CLOSED

THE SHOE STORE WENT OUT
OF BUSINESS BECAUSE NOT
ENOUGH PEOPLE ----

Now arrange the circled letters
to form the surprise answer, as
suggested by the above cartoon.

*Print
answer
here*

JUMBLE®

Unscramble these four Jumbles, one letter
to each square, to form four ordinary words.

NEFEC

DNYIK

TXOPER

LIGFIN

What is it like to
be identical twins?

I dunno. It's just
the way we are.
We're used to it.

WHEN ASKED ABOUT HOW
IDENTICAL THEY WERE, THE
TWINS WERE IDENTICALLY ----

Now arrange the circled letters
to form the surprise answer, as
suggested by the above cartoon.

Print
answer
here

JUMBLE®

Unscramble these four Jumbles, one letter to each square, to form four ordinary words.

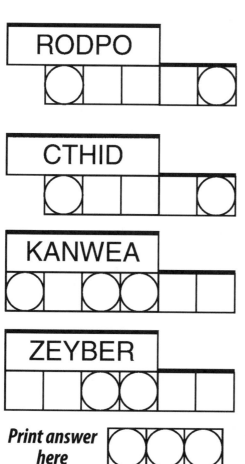

RODPO

CTHID

KANWEA

ZEYBER

Well, I've climbed all the big ones now. I guess I'm finished.

If you get to Mars, you could climb Olympus Mons.

AFTER REACHING EVEREST'S SUMMIT, HE FELT THAT HIS MOUNTAIN-CLIMBING CAREER----

Now arrange the circled letters to form the surprise answer, as suggested by the above cartoon.

Print answer here

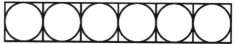

JUMBLE®

Unscramble these four Jumbles, one letter
to each square, to form four ordinary words.

MERIG

OHDUN

PITPEO

LHITPG

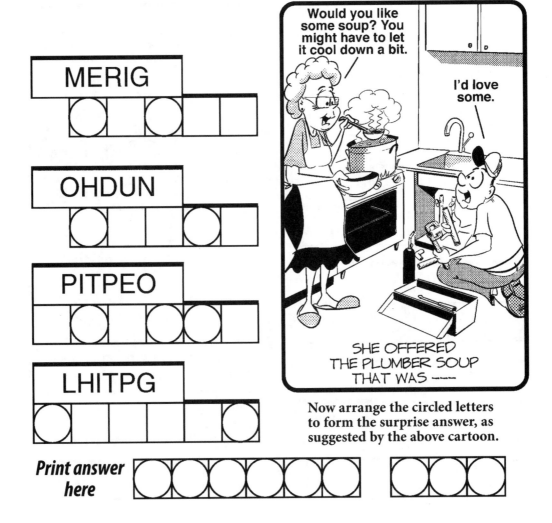

Would you like
some soup? You
might have to let
it cool down a bit.

I'd love
some.

SHE OFFERED
THE PLUMBER SOUP
THAT WAS —---

Now arrange the circled letters
to form the surprise answer, as
suggested by the above cartoon.

**Print answer
here**

JUMBLE®

Unscramble these four Jumbles, one letter to each square, to form four ordinary words.

RNETD

GULEN

TAGEEN

TIRRAY

IN 1927, GOING TO SEE "THE JAZZ SINGER" IN A THEATER WAS A ———

Now arrange the circled letters to form the surprise answer, as suggested by the above cartoon.

Print answer " ☐☐☐☐ " ☐☐☐☐☐

JUMBLE®

Unscramble these four Jumbles, one letter
to each square, to form four ordinary words.

AREMF

IVCCI

ANSOSE

TAUQIN

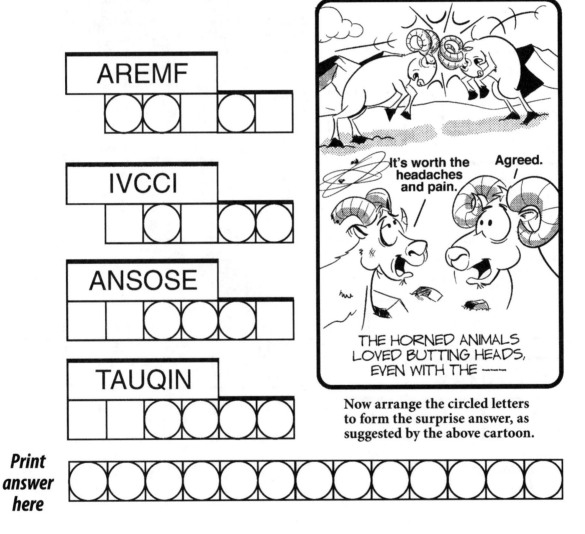

It's worth the headaches and pain.

Agreed.

THE HORNED ANIMALS
LOVED BUTTING HEADS,
EVEN WITH THE ———

Now arrange the circled letters
to form the surprise answer, as
suggested by the above cartoon.

Print answer here

JUMBLE®

Unscramble these four Jumbles, one letter
to each square, to form four ordinary words.

ZEBAL

YINAR

GMOYSG

SLUDHO

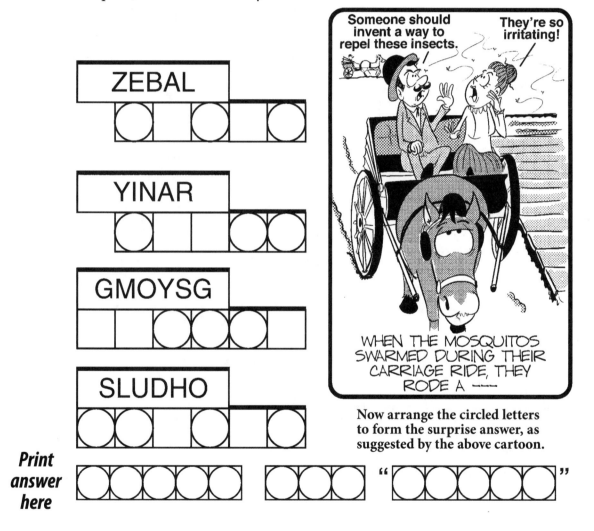

Someone should
invent a way to
repel these insects.

They're so
irritating!

WHEN THE MOSQUITOS
SWARMED DURING THEIR
CARRIAGE RIDE, THEY
RODE A ---

Now arrange the circled letters
to form the surprise answer, as
suggested by the above cartoon.

**Print
answer
here**

" "

JUMBLE®

Unscramble these four Jumbles, one letter to each square, to form four ordinary words.

MISUN

WOSNY

LCHIFN

CATPEK

Print answer here

How did you get out?

This will be my greatest performance.

AFTER ESCAPING HIS "UNDERWATER CELL," HOUDINI COULDN'T ---

Now arrange the circled letters to form the surprise answer, as suggested by the above cartoon.

70

JUMBLE®

Unscramble these four Jumbles, one letter to each square, to form four ordinary words.

FUTSF

RULTY

TARMET

CEERTJ

What arrr you doing with our booty?

The port is building new docks for you all.

TO COLLECT TAXES, THE PIRATE GOVERNMENT STARTED A ----

Now arrange the circled letters to form the surprise answer, as suggested by the above cartoon.

Print answer here ◯◯◯◯◯◯◯◯◯

JUMBLE®

Unscramble these four Jumbles, one letter
to each square, to form four ordinary words.

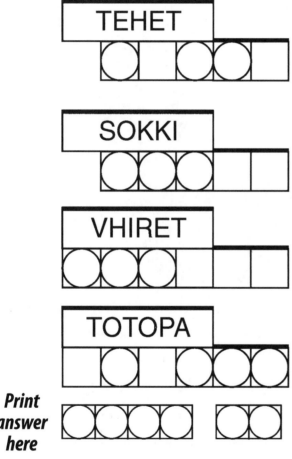

TEHET

SOKKI

VHIRET

TOTOPA

THE PATIENT WAS TOLD
TO LOWER HIS BLOOD
PRESSURE, AND HE ---

Now arrange the circled letters
to form the surprise answer, as
suggested by the above cartoon.

*Print
answer
here*

JUMBLE®

Unscramble these four Jumbles, one letter
to each square, to form four ordinary words.

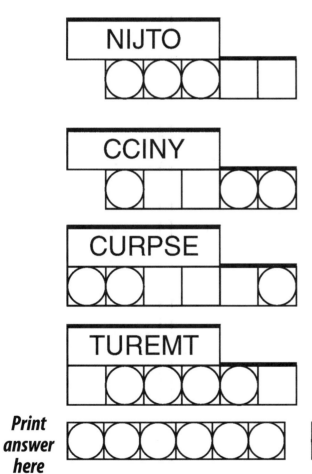

NIJTO

CCINY

CURPSE

TUREMT

You thought you were a sneak,
now you have the right not to speak.
So watch what you say,
or the court will make you pay.

Are you trying
to be funny?

THE RHYMING SHERIFF
SPECIALIZED IN ---

Now arrange the circled letters
to form the surprise answer, as
suggested by the above cartoon.

*Print
answer
here*

JUMBLE®

Unscramble these four Jumbles, one letter
to each square, to form four ordinary words.

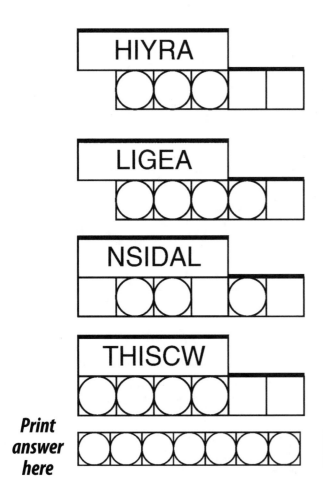

HIYRA

LIGEA

NSIDAL

THISCW

I'll go, but I don't know what good it'll do.

Like it or not, we need to have an estate plan.

SHE WANTED HIM TO GO WITH HER TO AN ESTATE PLANNER, AND HE DID IT ---

Now arrange the circled letters
to form the surprise answer, as
suggested by the above cartoon.

*Print
answer
here*

JUMBLE®

Unscramble these four Jumbles, one letter to each square, to form four ordinary words.

ZEAGU

RROMU

RILPSA

SLIVEW

What are we?

You're the best, Diana! I hope to hear all your hits tonight.

You're too kind.

WHEN IT CAME TO BEING A LEAD SINGER, DIANA ROSS WAS ----

Now arrange the circled letters to form the surprise answer, as suggested by the above cartoon.

Print answer here

JUMBLE®

Unscramble these four Jumbles, one letter
to each square, to form four ordinary words.

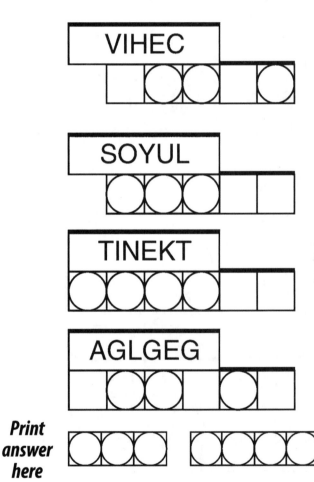

VIHEC

SOYUL

TINEKT

AGLGEG

He's been up
since sunrise
showing these off.

No wonder he
fell asleep so
quickly.

AFTER A LONG DAY OF
SHOWING OFF HIS NEW
ELECTRIC BULB, THOMAS
EDISON WAS ----

Now arrange the circled letters
to form the surprise answer, as
suggested by the above cartoon.

*Print
answer
here*

76

JUMBLE®

Unscramble these four Jumbles, one letter
to each square, to form four ordinary words.

CITHH

REEMG

PURYYS

CNECAT

What's the
asking price?

The owners
are moving
south.

FOR
SALE
GREAT VIEWS

THE FLOCK OF BIRDS
WAS SELLING ITS ROOSTS
AND HOPED THAT OTHER
BIRDS WOULD ---

Now arrange the circled letters
to form the surprise answer, as
suggested by the above cartoon.

**Print
answer
here**   " ◯◯◯◯◯◯◯ "   ◯◯◯◯

77

JUMBLE®

Unscramble these four Jumbles, one letter
to each square, to form four ordinary words.

HNICC

DOEMM

LOGMOY

SOKERH

May he rest in
peace in
heaven.

GEORGE V RULED BRITAIN
FROM 1910 UNTIL HE LEFT
FOR THIS IN 1936 ---

Now arrange the circled letters
to form the surprise answer, as
suggested by the above cartoon.

Print
answer
here

JUMBLE®

Unscramble these four Jumbles, one letter to each square, to form four ordinary words.

SOREA

ORDPO

TSELET

APFOYF

Here's to the love of my life. Thank you for saying yes to being my wife.

HE ASKED HER TO MARRY HIM, AND SHE SAID, "YES." THEN HE ---

Now arrange the circled letters to form the surprise answer, as suggested by the above cartoon.

JUMBLE®

Unscramble these four Jumbles, one letter
to each square, to form four ordinary words.

NUYGO

GENBA

HBLEAR

PEIRLP

I'm starving!

Two, please.

We are full tonight.

THE NEW RESTAURANT IN
BUDAPEST DID WELL, THANKS
TO ALL THE ----

Now arrange the circled letters
to form the surprise answer, as
suggested by the above cartoon.

Print answer here

"⬭⬭⬭⬭⬭⬭⬭⬭" ⬭⬭⬭⬭⬭⬭

JUMBLE®

Unscramble these four Jumbles, one letter
to each square, to form four ordinary words.

SEYZT

UYTIN

ONEPIG

GARNDO

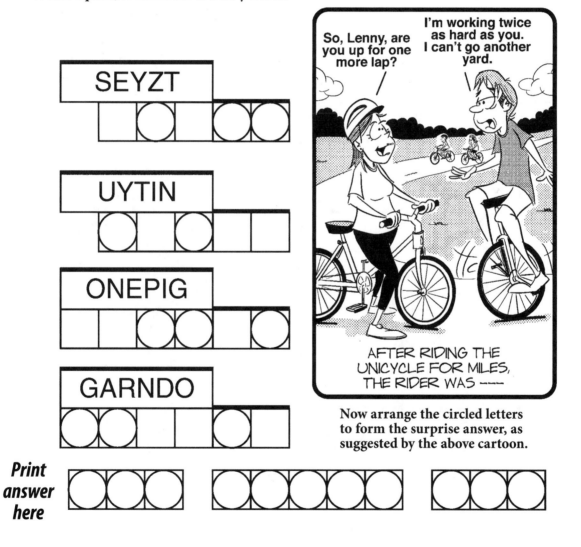

So, Lenny, are you up for one more lap?

I'm working twice as hard as you. I can't go another yard.

AFTER RIDING THE
UNICYCLE FOR MILES,
THE RIDER WAS ----

Now arrange the circled letters
to form the surprise answer, as
suggested by the above cartoon.

*Print
answer
here*

JUMBLE®

Unscramble these four Jumbles, one letter
to each square, to form four ordinary words.

SUYFS

EYEND

DIRZWA

EBELET

THE PEOPLE ON THE
PLATFORM WAVING
TO THE DEPARTING
TRAIN WERE ----

Now arrange the circled letters
to form the surprise answer, as
suggested by the above cartoon.

Print
answer
here

" ◯◯◯ - ◯◯◯◯◯◯◯◯◯ "

JUMBLE®

Unscramble these four Jumbles, one letter
to each square, to form four ordinary words.

REYVN

LAIEG

MOTYRS

KRASNH

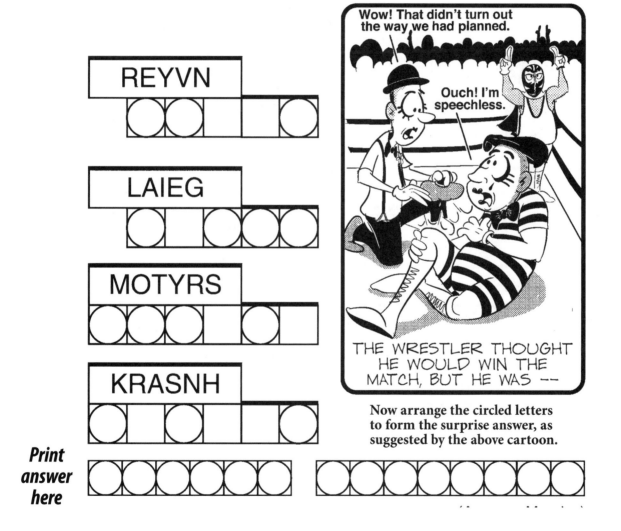

Wow! That didn't turn out
the way we had planned.

Ouch! I'm
speechless.

THE WRESTLER THOUGHT
HE WOULD WIN THE
MATCH, BUT HE WAS --

Now arrange the circled letters
to form the surprise answer, as
suggested by the above cartoon.

**Print
answer
here**

JUMBLE®

Unscramble these four Jumbles, one letter
to each square, to form four ordinary words.

ROSNW

WOYHD

PAYSPN

KENUBR

Looks like I
have a new
leader.

He
did
it!

IN A RACE WITH ANOTHER
REINDEER, RUDOLPH ----

Now arrange the circled letters
to form the surprise answer, as
suggested by the above cartoon.

Print
answer
here

JUMBLE®

Unscramble these four Jumbles, one letter
to each square, to form four ordinary words.

CAINP

KRELC

SLAVYT

HWOTNR

It's great that the national club is reading the same book.

I'm glad we can get together here in town to discuss it.

I couldn't put it down.

I loved this part.

THE NEW NATIONAL BOOK CLUB HAD ---

Now arrange the circled letters
to form the surprise answer, as
suggested by the above cartoon.

Print answer here

85

Unscramble these four Jumbles, one letter
to each square, to form four ordinary words.

TYTKI

VICCI

GIDNIO

NIWONM

Everything
is so shiny
and new.

This
place is
perfect.

WHEN THE COIN-PRODUCTION
FACILITY WAS COMPLETED,
IT WAS IN ----

Now arrange the circled letters
to form the surprise answer, as
suggested by the above cartoon.

**Print
answer
here**

JUMBLE®

Unscramble these four Jumbles, one letter
to each square, to form four ordinary words.

HANEY

VARFO

TONINO

EPTREM

How was everything?

Perfect! We were thinking about it all day.

I'm buying tonight.

RESTAURANTS IN TOKYO
SELL SUSHI TO CUSTOMERS
WHO ----

Now arrange the circled letters
to form the surprise answer, as
suggested by the above cartoon.

Print answer here

JUMBLE®

Unscramble these four Jumbles, one letter
to each square, to form four ordinary words.

XEPLI

AOOCC

GIMSAT

TUBENA

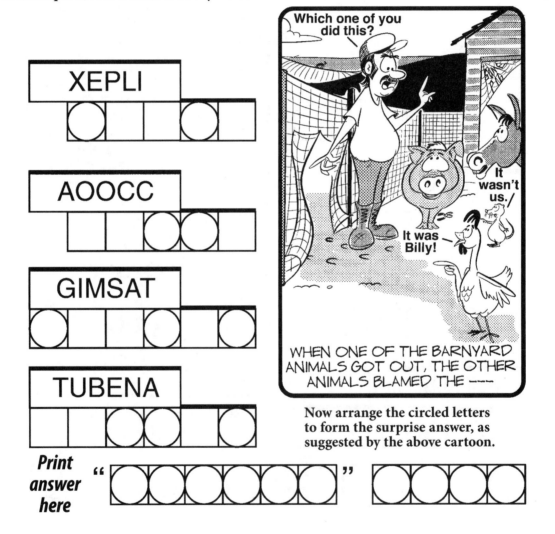

Which one of you did this?

It wasn't us.

It was Billy!

WHEN ONE OF THE BARNYARD
ANIMALS GOT OUT, THE OTHER
ANIMALS BLAMED THE ----

Now arrange the circled letters
to form the surprise answer, as
suggested by the above cartoon.

*Print
answer
here*   "⬡⬡⬡⬡⬡⬡⬡" ⬡⬡⬡⬡

JUMBLE®

Unscramble these four Jumbles, one letter
to each square, to form four ordinary words.

TICPH

ROURB

GIHYMT

FITANN

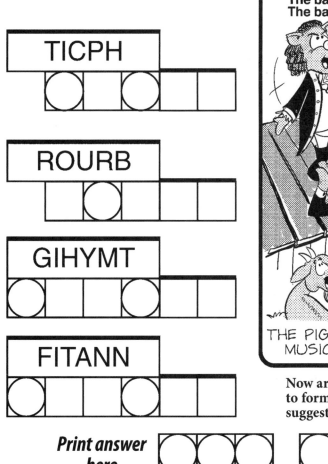

No one else was in
The barn where it happened
The barn where it happened

They just
keep topping
themselves.

THE PIGS WHO PUT ON THE
MUSICAL LOVED TO – – –

Now arrange the circled letters
to form the surprise answer, as
suggested by the above cartoon.

*Print answer
here*

JUMBLE®

Unscramble these four Jumbles, one letter to each square, to form four ordinary words.

JEYNO

GAILE

RRAATT

ASCION

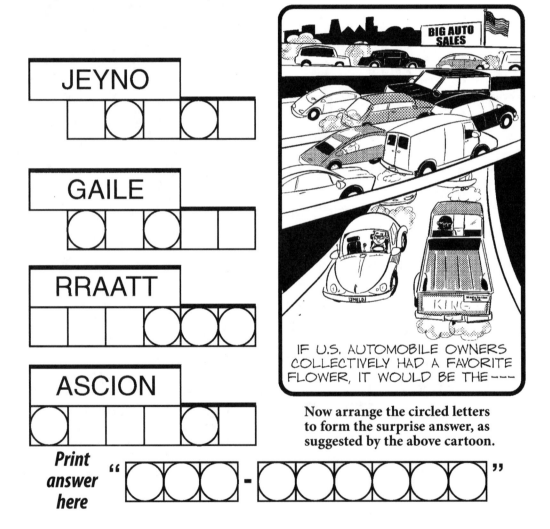

IF U.S. AUTOMOBILE OWNERS COLLECTIVELY HAD A FAVORITE FLOWER, IT WOULD BE THE ---

Now arrange the circled letters to form the surprise answer, as suggested by the above cartoon.

Print answer here " ◯◯◯ - ◯◯◯◯◯◯◯ "

JUMBLE®

Unscramble these four Jumbles, one letter
to each square, to form four ordinary words.

NVIGE

NGDAL

NIWOWD

LRHYAD

Coming right up.

I'll take another, please.

THE ARM WRESTLER WAS
ABOUT TO WIN AND HAD
THE MATCH ---

Now arrange the circled letters
to form the surprise answer, as
suggested by the above cartoon.

Print answer here

JUMBLE®

Unscramble these four Jumbles, one letter
to each square, to form four ordinary words.

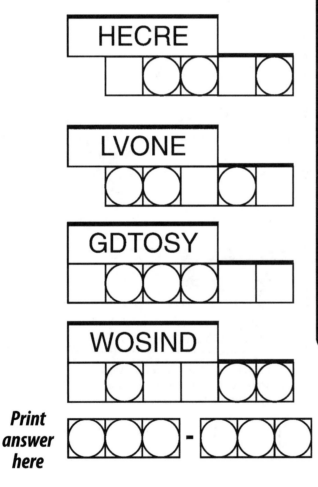

HECRE

LVONE

GDTOSY

WOSIND

There she
goes
again!

That's
why she
has such
a high
batting
average.

THE SUPERHERO WAS A
STAR ON HER SOFTBALL
TEAM AND NOT A ---

Now arrange the circled letters
to form the surprise answer, as
suggested by the above cartoon.

*Print
answer
here*

JUMBLE®

Unscramble these four Jumbles, one letter
to each square, to form four ordinary words.

PORAN

SITOH

RETVDI

CRAEDA

You've been pacing out in the hall. What can I do for you?

Um. Well, I was thinking something.

HE WANTED TO BRING UP THE
SUBJECT OF A PAY INCREASE
BUT WAS AFRAID TO ----

Now arrange the circled letters
to form the surprise answer, as
suggested by the above cartoon.

Print
answer
here

93

JUMBLE®

Unscramble these four Jumbles, one letter
to each square, to form four ordinary words.

COEUN

FINKE

DDOCEE

TZYLIG

Is this a joke?
Am I on a
hidden-
camera
show?

No. I just
asked if you
had any salad
for dinner.

HE COULDN'T BELIEVE THE
YOUNG GOAT COULD TALK.
THEN THE YOUNG GOAT SAID ----

Now arrange the circled letters
to form the surprise answer, as
suggested by the above cartoon.

Print
answer
here

Unscramble these four Jumbles, one letter
to each square, to form four ordinary words.

VALCO

LAURR

DOLYNF

GALEGH

Would you like a few pointers on growing corn?

I'll tell you a thing or two. I've been growing corn longer than you.

WHEN THE FARMER CRITICIZED
HIS NEIGHBOR'S CORN CROP,
HE GOT – – – –

Now arrange the circled letters
to form the surprise answer, as
suggested by the above cartoon.

Print answer here

JUMBLE®

Unscramble these four Jumbles, one letter
to each square, to form four ordinary words.

GHIST

ZAMEA

SENLOS

CUTEKB

The Poseidon crew
will show you all
how to handle the
rough seas.

AS THE CRUISE SHIP ROCKED,
THE STRUGGLING CREW AND
PASSENGERS WERE ---

Now arrange the circled letters
to form the surprise answer, as
suggested by the above cartoon.

**Print
answer
here**

JUMBLE®

Unscramble these four Jumbles, one letter
to each square, to form four ordinary words.

LANAV

USEGS

REVUDO

TEELTK

Wow! I
saw this
from
blocks
away

Can
we
get
some?

LILY'S
LEMONADE

FRESH SQUEEZED
LEMONADE

THE LEMONADE SELLER
WANTED HER BUSINESS TO ---

Now arrange the circled letters
to form the surprise answer, as
suggested by the above cartoon.

Print answer here

JUMBLE®

Unscramble these four Jumbles, one letter to each square, to form four ordinary words.

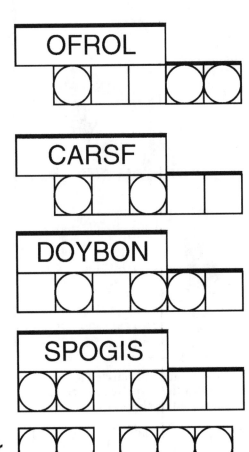

OFROL

CARSF

DOYBON

SPOGIS

How is it only seeing each other on the weekends?

It's OK. We talk online every day.

WHEN ASKED HOW HER LONG-DISTANCE RELATIONSHIP WAS GOING, SHE SAID ---

Now arrange the circled letters to form the surprise answer, as suggested by the above cartoon.

 Print answer here

 ,

JUMBLE®

Unscramble these four Jumbles, one letter
to each square, to form four ordinary words.

KEPYR

OTAIP

MIFYAL

UTPADE

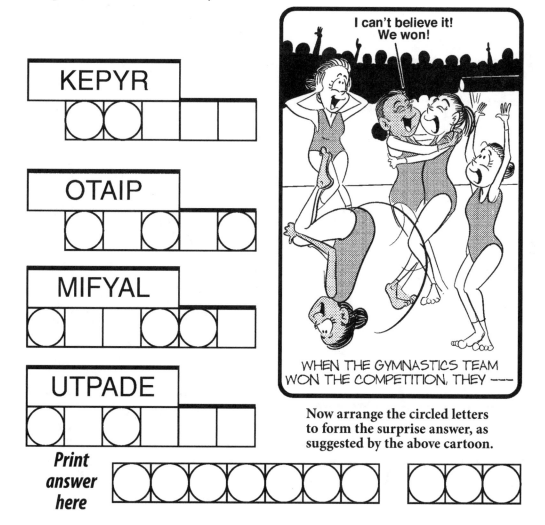

I can't believe it!
We won!

WHEN THE GYMNASTICS TEAM
WON THE COMPETITION, THEY ———

Now arrange the circled letters
to form the surprise answer, as
suggested by the above cartoon.

Print
answer
here

Unscramble these four Jumbles, one letter to each square, to form four ordinary words.

WETSE

VEOMI

SPLUCT

PRAROL

It's supposed to be of famous art.

This goes right there.

Remember this from Paris?

500

1,000

THE JIGSAW PUZZLES OF THE MONA LISA, DAVID AND VENUS DE MILO WERE ———

Now arrange the circled letters to form the surprise answer, as suggested by the above cartoon.

Print answer here

Unscramble these four Jumbles, one letter
to each square, to form four ordinary words.

CGOEK

LIDUF

STARHH

HANKES

I'm now in charge. We'll be doing things a little differently from now on.

Where's Mr. Dietz?

AFTER BECOMING A TEACHER IN SLEEPY HOLLOW, THE HORSEMAN WAS ---

Now arrange the circled letters
to form the surprise answer, as
suggested by the above cartoon.

*Print
answer
here*

JUMBLE®

Unscramble these four Jumbles, one letter
to each square, to form four ordinary words.

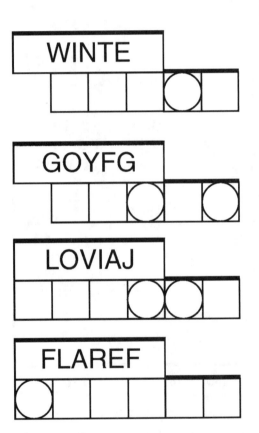

WINTE

GOYFG

LOVIAJ

FLAREF

I can't make anything out.

Let me try my camera.

THE FARMER TOOK A PHOTO
OF HIS WHEAT FIELD WITH
AN OLD CAMERA, BUT THE
PHOTO WAS – – –

Now arrange the circled letters
to form the surprise answer, as
suggested by the above cartoon.

Print answer here

102

JUMBLE®

Unscramble these four Jumbles, one letter to each square, to form four ordinary words.

TINAG

KREOB

KNIYNS

POTTIE

Don't wait up. I plan on making final table and winning tonight.

I'm pretty sure I'll be awake when you get home.

HE SAID HE WAS GOING TO WIN THE POKER TOURNAMENT, BUT HIS WIFE WASN'T ---

Now arrange the circled letters to form the surprise answer, as suggested by the above cartoon.

Print answer here

JUMBLE.

Unscramble these four Jumbles, one letter to each square, to form four ordinary words.

NORGP

LIHEW

PPUTEP

DISARH

What is it like exploring the deep seas?

The sea, once it casts its spell, holds one in its net of wonder forever.

Wow!

THE INTERVIEW WITH UNDERSEA-EXPLORER JACQUES COUSTEAU WAS ----

Now arrange the circled letters to form the surprise answer, as suggested by the above cartoon.

Print answer here ⬡⬡ - ⬡⬡⬡⬡⬡

JUMBLE®

Unscramble these four Jumbles, one letter to each square, to form four ordinary words.

XTOCI

RUYRH

SLUBEH

DUNOFE

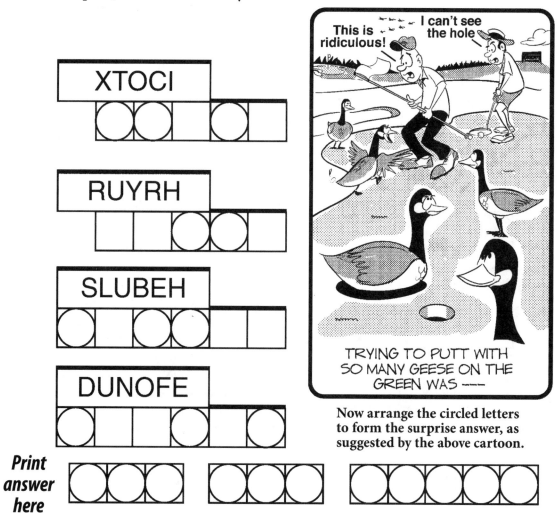

This is ridiculous!

I can't see the hole

TRYING TO PUTT WITH SO MANY GEESE ON THE GREEN WAS ----

Now arrange the circled letters to form the surprise answer, as suggested by the above cartoon.

Print answer here

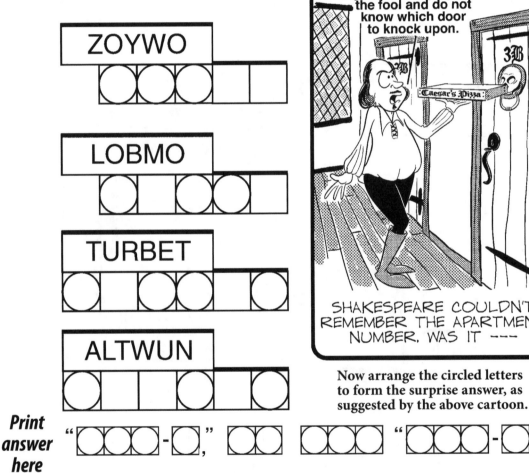

JUMBLE®

Unscramble these four Jumbles, one letter to each square, to form four ordinary words.

ZOYWO

LOBMO

TURBET

ALTWUN

This gives me pause. I am playing the fool and do not know which door to knock upon.

SHAKESPEARE COULDN'T REMEMBER THE APARTMENT NUMBER. WAS IT ---

Now arrange the circled letters to form the surprise answer, as suggested by the above cartoon.

Print answer here " ◯◯◯-◯ , " ◯◯ ◯◯◯ " ◯◯◯-◯ " ?

JUMBLE®

Unscramble these four Jumbles, one letter
to each square, to form four ordinary words.

COREF

KNALY

UDETOX

SHMIWY

It is the windiest continent. It is also home to about 70 percent of the planet's fresh water.

Why is it off the map?

BEING AT THE BOTTOM OF MOST MAPS, YOU NEED TO LOOK DOWN TO SEE ANTARCTICA'S – – –

Now arrange the circled letters
to form the surprise answer, as
suggested by the above cartoon.

*Print
answer
here* " ☐☐☐ - ☐☐☐☐☐☐ "

JUMBLE®

Unscramble these four Jumbles, one letter to each square, to form four ordinary words.

GALEE

RIHWL

GENCAY

DAYLLG

Donald, the doctor will see you now.

Just be patient.

THE VET THAT SPECIALIZED IN TREATING WATERFOWL HAD A ----

Now arrange the circled letters to form the surprise answer, as suggested by the above cartoon.

Print answer here " ◯◯◯◯◯◯ " ◯◯◯◯

JUMBLE®

Unscramble these four Jumbles, one letter
to each square, to form four ordinary words.

LERED

UNRET

MOLCRA

ALLUWF

The winners of the new windows are the Joneses.

WINDOW GIVEAWAY! DRAWING TODAY!

We won! That's one thing we won't have to worry about paying for.

Oh well.

AFTER WINNING NEW WINDOWS AT THE GRAND OPENING, THEY OWNED THEM ---

Now arrange the circled letters
to form the surprise answer, as
suggested by the above cartoon.

*Print
answer
here*

JUMBLE®

Unscramble these four Jumbles, one letter
to each square, to form four ordinary words.

YLURC

CRUKT

MIRADE

GOLANL

This piece was once
owned by Beyoncé.
She sold it to me.

Beyoncé?
Sold this to
you? Really?

THE STORY ABOUT THE
DIAMOND AND ITS
SETTING DIDN'T ---

Now arrange the circled letters
to form the surprise answer, as
suggested by the above cartoon.

*Print answer
here*

JUMBLE®

Unscramble these four Jumbles, one letter
to each square, to form four ordinary words.

LDAAS

PUTIL

COSTEK

SIFLOS

That's your cover?
Why don't you ever
have fun covers?

It's for
Presidents
Day. I can't
take your
editions
seriously.

You two
need to
work
things
out.

THE MAGAZINE'S EMPLOYEES
DIDN'T WORK WELL
TOGETHER AND HAD ---

Now arrange the circled letters
to form the surprise answer, as
suggested by the above cartoon.

Print
answer
here

JUMBLE®

Unscramble these four Jumbles, one letter
to each square, to form four ordinary words.

GINAA

UEEDX

FRACYT

NIPTUD

And there is Claire Haasl and David Hoyt.

Looks like every-body is here.

ALL THE STUDENTS AT THE
SCHOOL PROM WERE IN ----

Now arrange the circled letters
to form the surprise answer, as
suggested by the above cartoon.

Print answer here " ◯◯◯◯◯◯ - ◯◯◯◯◯ "

Unscramble these four Jumbles, one letter
to each square, to form four ordinary words.

FRADW

TOSOD

NOHHOC

THURCC

I'm the
number of
days in a
week!

What am I?
Nothing?

Well, I'm
greater
than
you!

THE SEVEN AND NINE
DIDN'T GET ALONG
AND WERE OFTEN ----

Now arrange the circled letters
to form the surprise answer, as
suggested by the above cartoon.

Print answer here

JUMBLE®

Unscramble these four Jumbles, one letter
to each square, to form four ordinary words.

CIHNF

RARUL

DEMLID

ACRAME

How's it feel, sir?

This is the executive version.

We need these in the boardroom.

THE HEAD OF THE RECLINER
FACTORY WAS THE ----

Now arrange the circled letters
to form the surprise answer, as
suggested by the above cartoon.

Print answer here

114

Unscramble these four Jumbles, one letter
to each square, to form four ordinary words.

TYEPT

ORNHO

SMUFOA

LAMCYL

I think a few of
you could have
done a little better.

How'd
you do?

C minus. I totally
studied for this.
My parents are
going to freak.

HE DIDN'T DO SO WELL ON
HIS ALGEBRA TEST AND
WORRIED ABOUT THE ---

Now arrange the circled letters
to form the surprise answer, as
suggested by the above cartoon.

Print answer here

JUMBLE®

Unscramble these four Jumbles, one letter to each square, to form four ordinary words.

FINKE

TBUDO

GONLOA

SSUIME

We knew it!

Gotcha!

THE SKUNKS KNEW EXACTLY WHEN TO SPRAY, THANKS TO ---

Now arrange the circled letters to form the surprise answer, as suggested by the above cartoon.

Print answer here ☐☐☐☐ " ☐☐-☐☐☐☐☐☐ "

Unscramble these four Jumbles, one letter
to each square, to form four ordinary words.

LUFTA

CROPH

BYDIRH

EDENEL

They need
you on top!
Jefferson's face
has cracks in it!

Tell them I'm
on my way.

MOUNT RUSHMORE'S
SUPERVISOR WAS NEEDED,
SO HE PREPARED TO ---

Now arrange the circled letters
to form the surprise answer, as
suggested by the above cartoon.

Print
answer
here

JUMBLE®

Unscramble these four Jumbles, one letter
to each square, to form four ordinary words.

SUHEO

COKOR

TEPTIE

CCSTAU

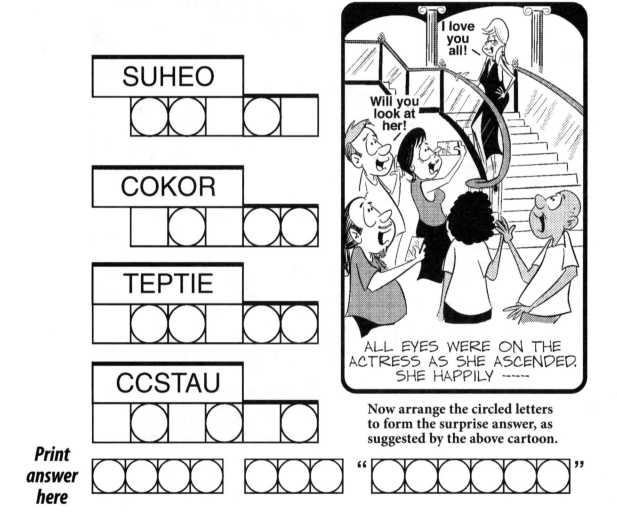

I love
you
all!

Will you
look at
her!

ALL EYES WERE ON THE
ACTRESS AS SHE ASCENDED.
SHE HAPPILY ----

Now arrange the circled letters
to form the surprise answer, as
suggested by the above cartoon.

Print
answer
here

"   "

JUMBLE®

Unscramble these four Jumbles, one letter
to each square, to form four ordinary words.

NAXEN

RYIDT

POLPTA

RUMMUR

This is crazy!

Every time!

Hi-yah!

Bring it!

WHEN THE GIANT ANIMALS
ARGUED OVER BAMBOO,
THE RESULT WAS ---

Now arrange the circled letters
to form the surprise answer, as
suggested by the above cartoon.

Print
answer
here

" ◯◯◯◯◯◯ - ◯◯◯◯◯◯ "

JUMBLE®

Unscramble these four Jumbles, one letter
to each square, to form four ordinary words.

FAYDF

CREWK

EERRTV

SABPYS

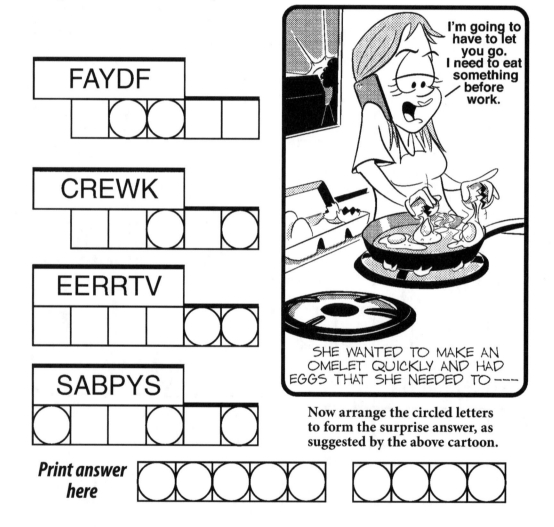

I'm going to have to let you go. I need to eat something before work.

SHE WANTED TO MAKE AN OMELET QUICKLY AND HAD EGGS THAT SHE NEEDED TO ---

Now arrange the circled letters
to form the surprise answer, as
suggested by the above cartoon.

Print answer
here

120

JUMBLE®

Unscramble these four Jumbles, one letter
to each square, to form four ordinary words.

NASDT

VARLA

GERRUB

FRUGIE

Do you think this looks good?

It's perfect!

HE WAS GOING TO A BLACK-
TIE EVENT AND NEEDED AN
OUTFIT THAT WAS---

Now arrange the circled letters
to form the surprise answer, as
suggested by the above cartoon.

Print answer here

JUMBLE®

Unscramble these four Jumbles, one letter to each square, to form four ordinary words.

GDUNE

BEAAT

CPRITS

LETYAL

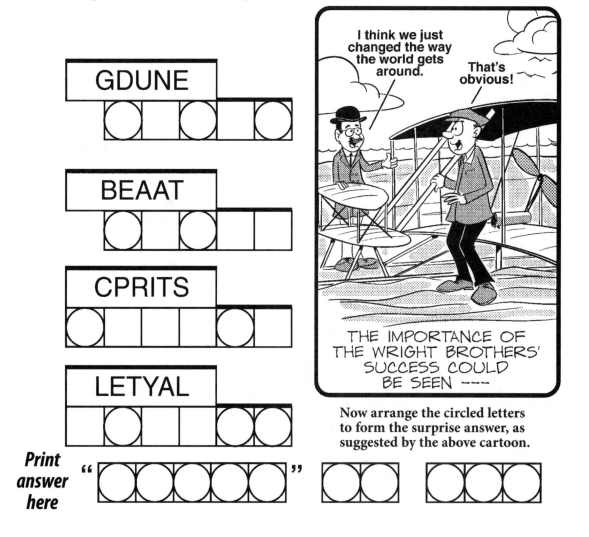

I think we just changed the way the world gets around.

That's obvious!

THE IMPORTANCE OF THE WRIGHT BROTHERS' SUCCESS COULD BE SEEN ----

Now arrange the circled letters to form the surprise answer, as suggested by the above cartoon.

Print answer here

" ◯◯◯◯◯ " ◯◯ ◯◯◯

JUMBLE®

Unscramble these four Jumbles, one letter to each square, to form four ordinary words.

WHOSN

PDATA

FDTEEC

WRTTEE

My sculpture's interactive program will answer any questions about Alaska. It even has Bluetooth.

Wow! That's high-tech!

Show me Juneau.

THE HIGH-TECH SCULPTURE OF ALASKA WAS ---

Now arrange the circled letters to form the surprise answer, as suggested by the above cartoon.

Print answer here

JUMBLE®

Unscramble these four Jumbles, one letter to each square, to form four ordinary words.

BRONI

RHAWF

TPOYER

GLUEED

Olga! We're back from our journey!

How was the pillaging?

THE VIKINGS WERE JUST ABOUT HOME AFTER A LONG ----

Now arrange the circled letters to form the surprise answer, as suggested by the above cartoon.

Print answer here "◯◯◯◯◯" ◯◯◯◯

JUMBLE®

Unscramble these four Jumbles, one letter
to each square, to form four ordinary words.

GOYSG

GODED

PCRANE

GUTENG

I thought
they were
finished
last week.

It broke
down
again.

THE INSTALLATION OF
THE CITY'S NEW TRAFFIC
LIGHT WAS ---

Now arrange the circled letters
to form the surprise answer, as
suggested by the above cartoon.

**Print
answer
here**

◯◯◯◯ - ◯◯◯ - ◯◯

JUMBLE®

Unscramble these four Jumbles, one letter
to each square, to form four ordinary words.

DONPU

HYYLS

CLIPEO

REBYEZ

So where
did you
fly?

I flew
volcano
tours in
Hawaii.

THE HELICOPTER PILOT WHO
BECAME A CHEF WAS A ----

Now arrange the circled letters
to form the surprise answer, as
suggested by the above cartoon.

Print answer here

JUMBLE®

Unscramble these four Jumbles, one letter
to each square, to form four ordinary words.

YTAFT

SDERS

DPERAA

TAVCIE

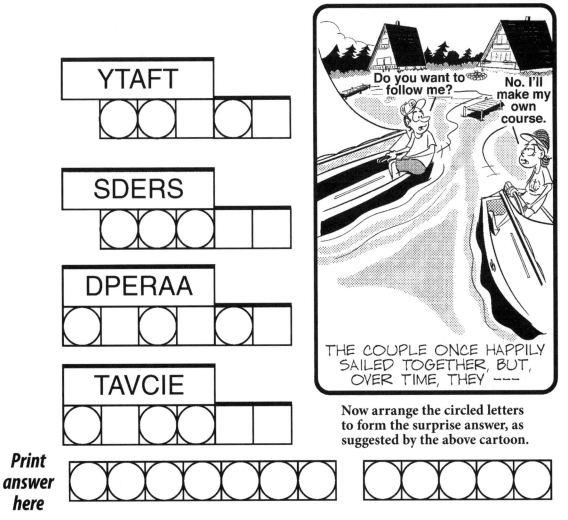

Do you want to follow me?

No. I'll make my own course.

THE COUPLE ONCE HAPPILY
SAILED TOGETHER, BUT,
OVER TIME, THEY ---

Now arrange the circled letters
to form the surprise answer, as
suggested by the above cartoon.

Print
answer
here

JUMBLE®

Unscramble these four Jumbles, one letter to each square, to form four ordinary words.

LAYEL

IZEES

EBOWLB

COVIRT

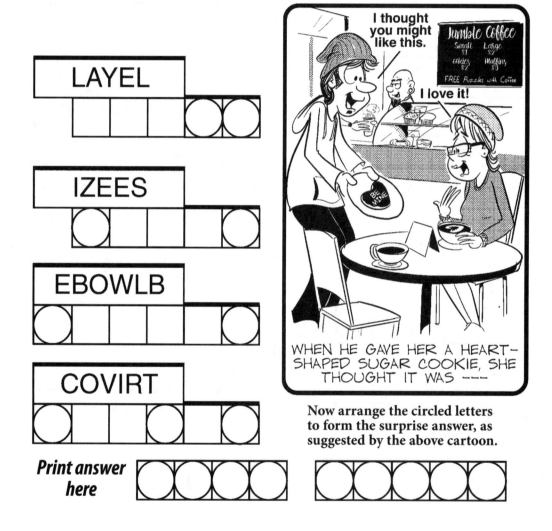

I thought you might like this.

Jumble Coffee
Small $1 Large $4
Cookies $2 Muffins $3
FREE Puzzles with Coffee

I love it!

BE MINE

WHEN HE GAVE HER A HEART-SHAPED SUGAR COOKIE, SHE THOUGHT IT WAS ---

Now arrange the circled letters to form the surprise answer, as suggested by the above cartoon.

Print answer here

128

JUMBLE®

Unscramble these four Jumbles, one letter to each square, to form four ordinary words.

NGUTS

VLAHE

BRMEAK

GUMSPY

The thrill is gone away from me Although, I'll still live on But so lonely I'll be

I can't believe he's gone.

It's so sad.

WHEN B.B. KING PASSED AWAY IN 2015, HIS FANS ----

Now arrange the circled letters to form the surprise answer, as suggested by the above cartoon.

Print answer here

JUMBLE®

Unscramble these four Jumbles, one letter
to each square, to form four ordinary words.

LITET

TLASN

TAVLYS

EGNEVA

THEY KNEW THE TIME OF
THE AUTHOR'S READING
BECAUSE OF THE ---

Now arrange the circled letters
to form the surprise answer, as
suggested by the above cartoon.

Print
answer
here

JUMBLE®

Unscramble these four Jumbles, one letter to each square, to form four ordinary words.

NIRWG

PLOEE

NETTNA

HEDNIB

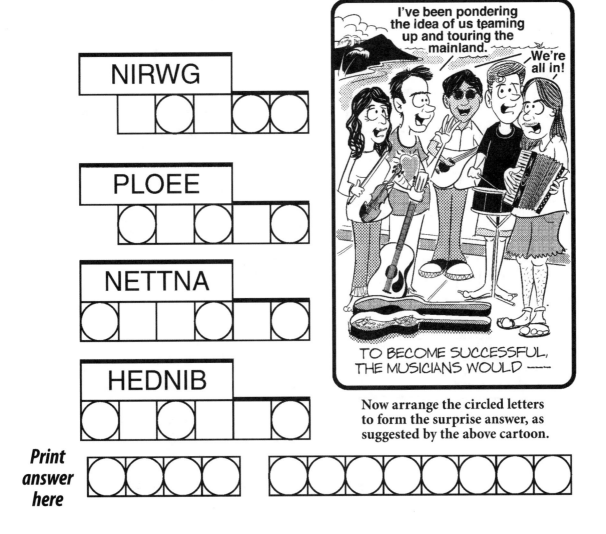

TO BECOME SUCCESSFUL, THE MUSICIANS WOULD ----

Now arrange the circled letters to form the surprise answer, as suggested by the above cartoon.

Print answer here

JUMBLE®

Unscramble these four Jumbles, one letter to each square, to form four ordinary words.

CAHWK

MHYET

GHIYET

GDISIN

This will be great on my next business trip.

"Namaste" to you too!

NAMASTE – Hindi
CIAO – Italian
HOLA – Spanish

THE APP THAT COULD TRANSLATE "HELLO" INTO ANY LANGUAGE WAS – – –

Now arrange the circled letters to form the surprise answer, as suggested by the above cartoon.

Print answer here "◯◯" - ◯◯◯◯◯

JUMBLE®

Unscramble these four Jumbles, one letter
to each square, to form four ordinary words.

OAKAL

VONWE

RWATDO

DRYEEE

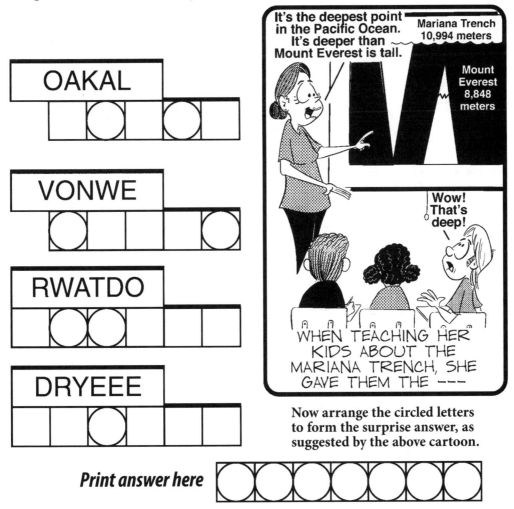

It's the deepest point
in the Pacific Ocean.
It's deeper than
Mount Everest is tall.

Mariana Trench
10,994 meters

Mount
Everest
8,848
meters

Wow!
That's
deep!

WHEN TEACHING HER
KIDS ABOUT THE
MARIANA TRENCH, SHE
GAVE THEM THE ---

Now arrange the circled letters
to form the surprise answer, as
suggested by the above cartoon.

Print answer here

JUMBLE®

Unscramble these four Jumbles, one letter
to each square, to form four ordinary words.

LAMAL

SOYBS

ELOSSN

OPITTE

I like what's going on here. Will it be ready for the runway?

Yes. But I'll be cutting it close.

WHEN ASKED IF SHE COULD FINISH THE DRESS IN AN HOUR, SHE SAID IT ---

Now arrange the circled letters
to form the surprise answer, as
suggested by the above cartoon.

Print answer here

" ◯◯◯◯◯ "   ◯◯◯◯◯◯◯◯◯

JUMBLE®

Unscramble these four Jumbles, one letter
to each square, to form four ordinary words.

SEMYS

SUDEO

CLHINF

DEBOYM

THE COMPANY COULDN'T
MAKE A PROFIT SELLING
ORIGAMI, SO THE ---

Now arrange the circled letters
to form the surprise answer, as
suggested by the above cartoon.

*Print
answer
here*

JUMBLE®

Unscramble these four Jumbles, one letter
to each square, to form four ordinary words.

RFOEF

CYITH

NIESUG

CANUNE

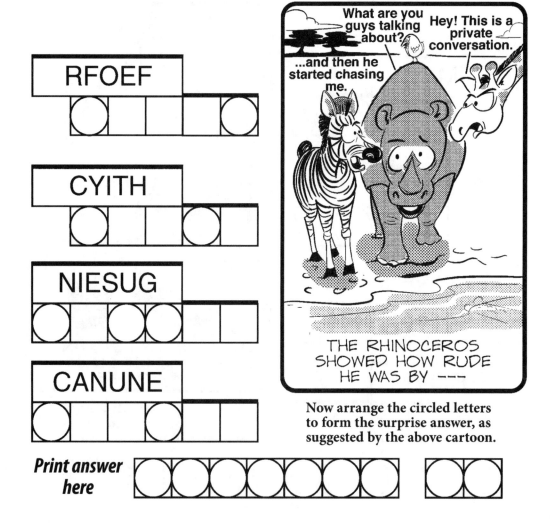

What are you guys talking about?

Hey! This is a private conversation.

...and then he started chasing me.

THE RHINOCEROS
SHOWED HOW RUDE
HE WAS BY ---

Now arrange the circled letters
to form the surprise answer, as
suggested by the above cartoon.

Print answer here

JUMBLE®

Unscramble these four Jumbles, one letter
to each square, to form four ordinary words.

WERVA

PYHPA

TTEEKL

CASECS

Our files show
that you shared
"Love Is..." cartoons
without the copyright
information.

That
was years
ago!

Bill King
Mac King's
Magic in a Minute

GUEST
JUMBLER
SELECTION
COMMITTEE

THE BACKGROUND CHECK
ON THE CARTOONIST
SHOWED THAT HE HAD A ---

Now arrange the circled letters
to form the surprise answer, as
suggested by the above cartoon.

Print
answer
here

137

JUMBLE®

Unscramble these four Jumbles, one letter to each square, to form four ordinary words.

TEADD

PLMIB

RUUYXL

BYRRUL

Ouch!

That's what you get for not paying attention.

Idiot!

THE WEIGHTLIFTER WHO DROPPED THE WEIGHT ON HIS FOOT WAS A ---

Now arrange the circled letters to form the surprise answer, as suggested by the above cartoon.

Print answer here

138

JUMBLE®

Unscramble these four Jumbles, one letter to each square, to form four ordinary words.

DLNAB

NORGP

RMILEB

SCUACE

May I take your orders?

I miss giving orders.

I miss the officers' club.

Alice's Restaurant

I've got to be home at 1300 hours.

THE FOUR-STAR MILITARY COMMANDERS RETIRED AND BECAME PART OF THE ---

Now arrange the circled letters to form the surprise answer, as suggested by the above cartoon.

Print answer here

JUMBLE®

Unscramble these four Jumbles, one letter
to each square, to form four ordinary words.

CONKK

SMURT

GIROIN

FBETUF

Here they
are at #1
again!
I love their
new look.

I love
seeing
what
they'll do
next.

WHEN IT CAME TO MUSIC
IN THE MID-1960s, THE
BEATLES WERE AT THE ---

Now arrange the circled letters
to form the surprise answer, as
suggested by the above cartoon.

Print
answer
here

"◯◯◯◯◯ - ◯◯◯◯◯◯"

JUMBLE®

Unscramble these four Jumbles, one letter
to each square, to form four ordinary words.

KNOTE

TCAFE

TULFIE

RASHSA

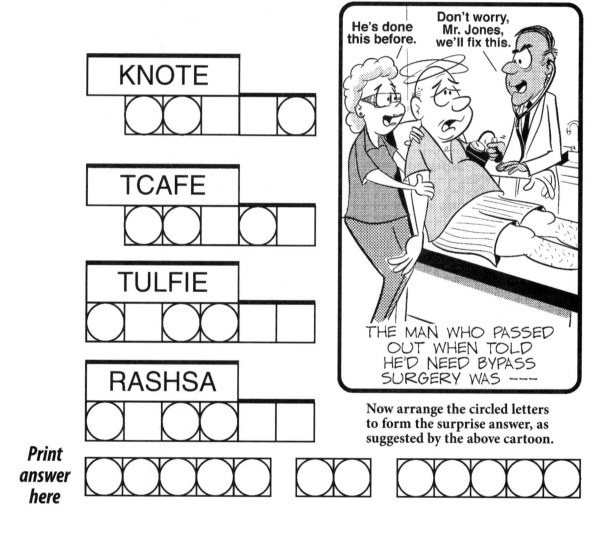

He's done
this before.

Don't worry,
Mr. Jones,
we'll fix this.

THE MAN WHO PASSED
OUT WHEN TOLD
HE'D NEED BYPASS
SURGERY WAS ---

Now arrange the circled letters
to form the surprise answer, as
suggested by the above cartoon.

Print
answer
here

JUMBLE®

Unscramble these four Jumbles, one letter
to each square, to form four ordinary words.

GOBYE

CLERI

RANDOW

SLALUC

Aren't you exhausted?
You won't need to go
to the gym after this
workout.

I know! I think
I've lost 5
pounds this
week.

TO GET ENOUGH
FIREWOOD TO WARM UP
THEIR HOME, HE ---

Now arrange the circled letters
to form the surprise answer, as
suggested by the above cartoon.

**Print
answer
here**

JUMBLE®

Unscramble these four Jumbles, one letter
to each square, to form four ordinary words.

DRUFA

LIEGA

GLIEPT

KENURB

And for about $800 million, you'll get the team and the stadium.

OK. But that's almost all of my lottery winnings.

THE TEAM WAS FOR SALE
FOR ABOUT $800 MILLION.
THE PRICE WAS A ---

Now arrange the circled letters
to form the surprise answer, as
suggested by the above cartoon.

Print
answer
here

143

JUMBLE®

Unscramble these four Jumbles, one letter to each square, to form four ordinary words.

NIHTK

FARET

MOSTOH

GULJEG

Print answer here

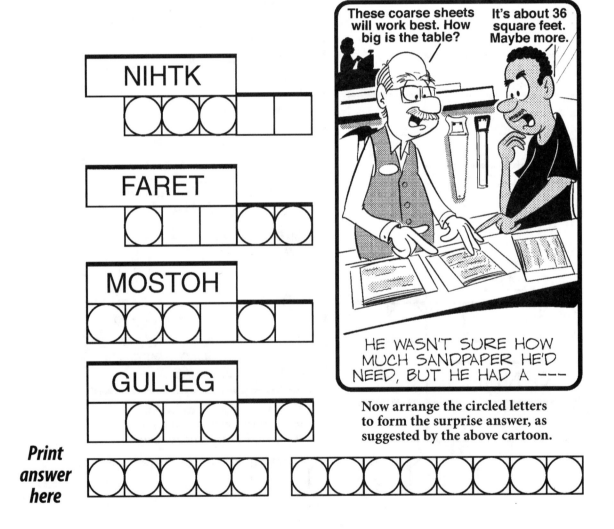

These coarse sheets will work best. How big is the table?

It's about 36 square feet. Maybe more.

HE WASN'T SURE HOW MUCH SANDPAPER HE'D NEED, BUT HE HAD A ---

Now arrange the circled letters to form the surprise answer, as suggested by the above cartoon.

JUMBLE®

Unscramble these four Jumbles, one letter to each square, to form four ordinary words.

NUWSG

RIHEK

CRUPES

CAYPFI

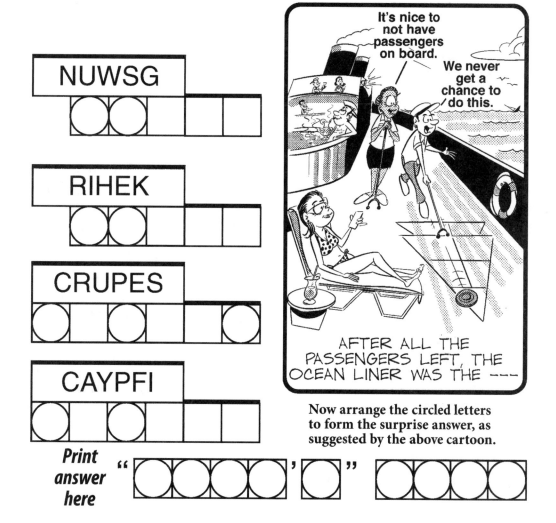

It's nice to not have passengers on board.

We never get a chance to do this.

AFTER ALL THE PASSENGERS LEFT, THE OCEAN LINER WAS THE ---

Now arrange the circled letters to form the surprise answer, as suggested by the above cartoon.

Print answer here " ◯◯◯◯ ' ◯ " ◯◯◯◯

JUMBLE®

Unscramble these four Jumbles, one letter
to each square, to form four ordinary words.

CHAHT

HURGS

MATIGS

NOIRUJ

You need to season them like mine!

You two need to get along and get me my orders.

Mine are fine! Yours are too salty.

AFTER FIGHTING OVER WHO MADE BETTER BREAKFAST POTATOES, THEY WOULD ---

Now arrange the circled letters
to form the surprise answer, as
suggested by the above cartoon.

Print
answer
here

JUMBLE®

Unscramble these four Jumbles, one letter to each square, to form four ordinary words.

RAHOD

NUDOH

SERDYS

TAREMU

I was sculpted first because I'm the father of the country! I helped create the republic!

Well, lah dee dah! I saved it. And that's the truth!

COMPETITION BETWEEN MOUNT RUSHMORE'S PRESIDENTS WAS ---

Now arrange the circled letters to form the surprise answer, as suggested by the above cartoon.

Print answer here

◯◯◯◯ - ◯◯ - ◯◯◯◯

JUMBLE®

Unscramble these four Jumbles, one letter to each square, to form four ordinary words.

KNOTE

FIRTD

SCEWHA

GOINGN

We are going to be full today. Lots on our agenda.

Where would you like the cruise ship parked?

THE HARBOR MASTER HAD A BUSY DAY SCHEDULED, WITH SEVERAL SHIPS ----

Now arrange the circled letters to form the surprise answer, as suggested by the above cartoon.

Print answer here ◯◯ ◯◯◯ " ◯◯◯◯◯ - ◯◯ "

JUMBLE®

Unscramble these four Jumbles, one letter
to each square, to form four ordinary words.

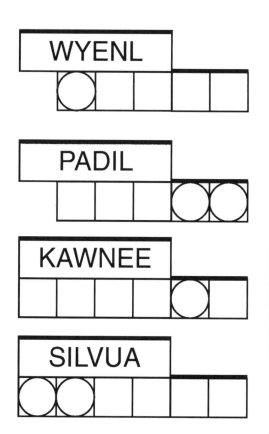

WYENL

PADIL

KAWNEE

SILVUA

> This harvest is wonderful.
>
> These are heavenly!

THE WINERY'S GRAPES WERE FINALLY READY TO PICK. THEY DESCRIBED THE TASTE AS ----

Now arrange the circled letters
to form the surprise answer, as
suggested by the above cartoon.

Print answer here

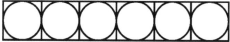

149

JUMBLE

Unscramble these four Jumbles, one letter
to each square, to form four ordinary words.

INOON

UNDOR

TEGRAH

FLUREF

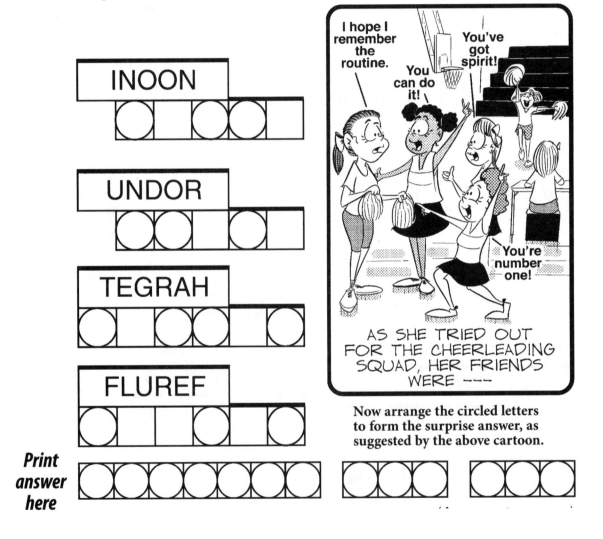

I hope I remember the routine.

You can do it!

You've got spirit!

You're number one!

AS SHE TRIED OUT
FOR THE CHEERLEADING
SQUAD, HER FRIENDS
WERE –––

Now arrange the circled letters
to form the surprise answer, as
suggested by the above cartoon.

Print
answer
here

JUMBLE®

Unscramble these four Jumbles, one letter
to each square, to form four ordinary words.

SINYO

YARLO

OTAGEE

GRETTA

I've got more
cheese for you.
Isn't this awesome?

Are
you
kidding
me?

THE PIZZA PARLOR'S EMPLOYEE
FOUND SHREDDING SO MUCH
CHEESE TO BE ---

Now arrange the circled letters
to form the surprise answer, as
suggested by the above cartoon.

Print answer here

JUMBLE®

Unscramble these four Jumbles, one letter
to each square, to form four ordinary words.

RAHHS

CRTAT

FEWLAF

OPSPEO

I can't find my glasses. I don't want to miss it.

It's amazing!

This is the best one I've seen!

DURING THE BIG ECLIPSE OF 2017, THE SUN WAS THE ---

Now arrange the circled letters
to form the surprise answer, as
suggested by the above cartoon.

*Print
answer
here*

JUMBLE®

Unscramble these four Jumbles, one letter
to each square, to form four ordinary words.

CATEU

TREXE

XREVOT

ARYPOD

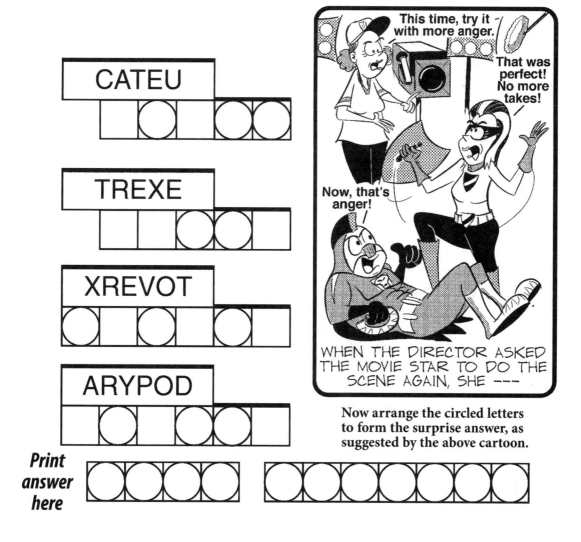

This time, try it with more anger.

That was perfect! No more takes!

Now, that's anger!

WHEN THE DIRECTOR ASKED THE MOVIE STAR TO DO THE SCENE AGAIN, SHE ---

Now arrange the circled letters
to form the surprise answer, as
suggested by the above cartoon.

*Print
answer
here*

JUMBLE®

Unscramble these four Jumbles, one letter to each square, to form four ordinary words.

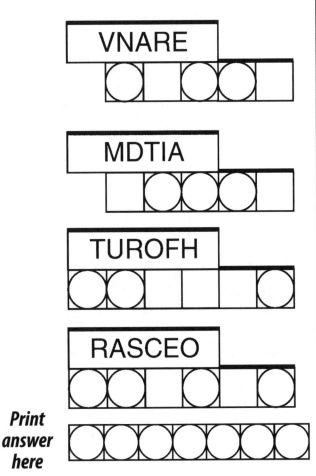

VNARE

MDTIA

TUROFH

RASCEO

Hey! Where's Bill?

He's sick. I can finish his job.

WHEN THE HOUSE PAINTER CALLED IN SICK, ANOTHER PAINTER ---

Now arrange the circled letters to form the surprise answer, as suggested by the above cartoon.

Print answer here

154

JUMBLE®

Unscramble these four Jumbles, one letter
to each square, to form four ordinary words.

GROOF

EELXI

HUGONE

STULEA

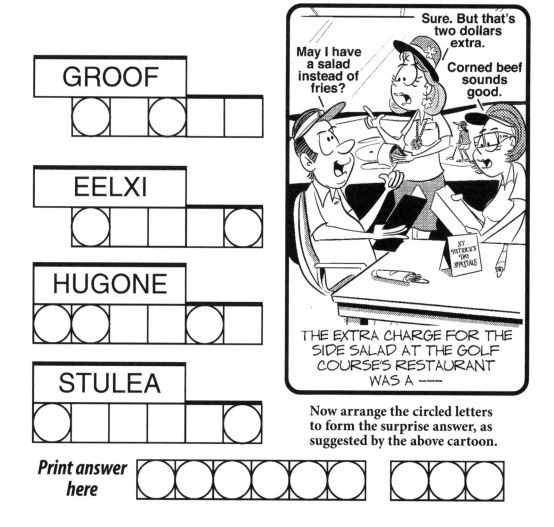

Sure. But that's
two dollars
extra.

May I have
a salad
instead of
fries?

Corned beef
sounds
good.

ST. PATRICK'S DAY SPECIALS

THE EXTRA CHARGE FOR THE
SIDE SALAD AT THE GOLF
COURSE'S RESTAURANT
WAS A ---

Now arrange the circled letters
to form the surprise answer, as
suggested by the above cartoon.

*Print answer
here*

JUMBLE®

Unscramble these four Jumbles, one letter
to each square, to form four ordinary words.

TOMEP

OLYRG

SINOIV

ROAPND

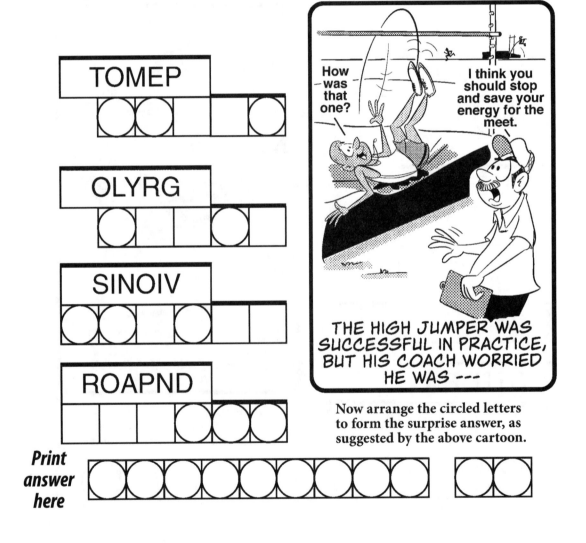

How was that one?

I think you should stop and save your energy for the meet.

THE HIGH JUMPER WAS
SUCCESSFUL IN PRACTICE,
BUT HIS COACH WORRIED
HE WAS ---

Now arrange the circled letters
to form the surprise answer, as
suggested by the above cartoon.

Print
answer
here

JUMBLE®

Unscramble these four Jumbles, one letter
to each square, to form four ordinary words.

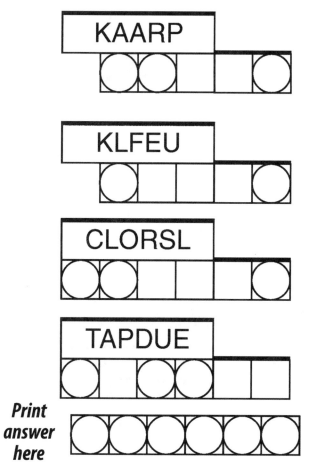

KAARP

KLFEU

CLORSL

TAPDUE

How did
that get in
here?

Are you
kidding
me?

Can I
keep
him?

THE BIRD THAT
ACCIDENTALLY FLEW
INSIDE THE HOUSE ---

Now arrange the circled letters
to form the surprise answer, as
suggested by the above cartoon.

Print
answer
here

157

JUMBLE®

Unscramble these four Jumbles, one letter to each square, to form four ordinary words.

CWAYK

DEALG

NURYHG

WDERHS

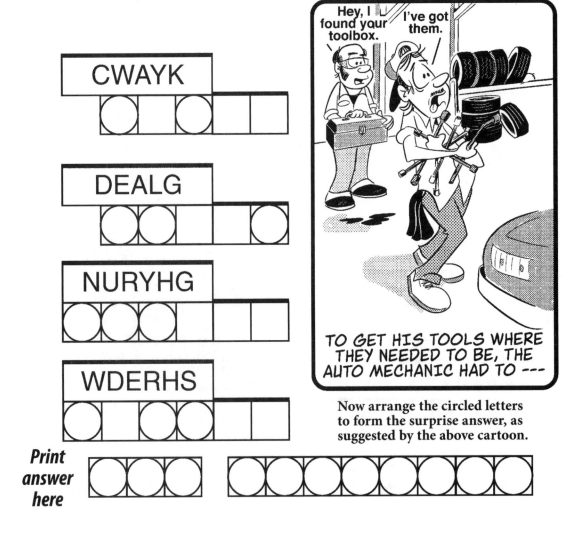

Hey, I found your toolbox.

I've got them.

TO GET HIS TOOLS WHERE THEY NEEDED TO BE, THE AUTO MECHANIC HAD TO ---

Now arrange the circled letters to form the surprise answer, as suggested by the above cartoon.

Print answer here

JUMBLE®

Unscramble these four Jumbles, one letter to each square, to form four ordinary words.

SATTY

VOLNE

RIHFTT

WKEYEL

Wow! Match point, already!

She's good.

King	6	5	45
Kent	0	0	0

THE TENNIS PLAYER HADN'T LOST A SINGLE GAME TO HER OPPONENT AND WAS ---

Now arrange the circled letters to form the surprise answer, as suggested by the above cartoon.

Print answer here

Unscramble these four Jumbles, one letter
to each square, to form four ordinary words.

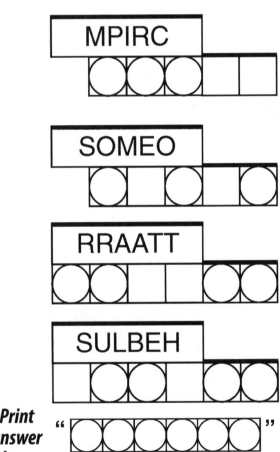

MPIRC

SOMEO

RRAATT

SULBEH

These canvas flags
will stand up to the
sea breeze much
better.

Pull the
stick, will
you?

IN THE EARLY DAYS OF
GOLF, THE FLAGS WERE
MADE OUT OF ---

Now arrange the circled letters
to form the surprise answer, as
suggested by the above cartoon.

*Print
answer
here*

JUMBLE®

Unscramble these four Jumbles, one letter
to each square, to form four ordinary words.

NUYNS

URRMO

BMMEEL

LUSODH

Our sales have been solid.

20,000   5,000

NORTH

WEST   EAST   10,000

SOUTH

15,000

Let's keep them rolling.

HULA-HOOP SALES
WERE REPORTED IN ---

Now arrange the circled letters
to form the surprise answer, as
suggested by the above cartoon.

Print
answer
here

161

JUMBLE®

Unscramble these four Jumbles, one letter to each square, to form four ordinary words.

GYANT

CANTE

TIRRYA

COYCUP

Ow! You little stinker.
You are lucky you're
so adorable.

WHEN THE KITTEN
SCRATCHED HER ARM,
SHE SUFFERED ---

Now arrange the circled letters to form the surprise answer, as suggested by the above cartoon.

Print answer here

" ☐-☐☐☐☐ " ☐☐☐☐

JUMBLE®

CHAMPION

Challenger
Puzzles

JUMBLE®

Unscramble these six Jumbles, one letter
to each square, to form six ordinary words.

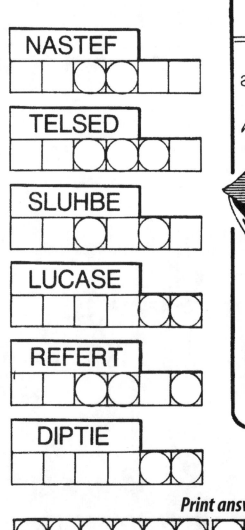

NASTEF

TELSED

SLUHBE

LUCASE

REFERT

DIPTIE

WEIGHT CONTROL

BOOKS

SLIM DOWN

THE BEST WEIGHT-
REDUCING DIET IS
ONE THAT MAKES
YOU DO THIS.

Now arrange the circled letters
to form the surprise answer, as
suggested by the above cartoon.

Print answer here

JUMBLE®

Unscramble these six Jumbles, one letter to each square, to form six ordinary words.

TENJIC

VAJILO

FRAGEO

ANZATS

DEKORF

BRILEM

WHAT THEY CALLED THE COURSE FOR APPRENTICE PLUMBERS.

Now arrange the circled letters to form the surprise answer, as suggested by the above cartoon.

Print answer here

◯◯◯◯◯ " ◯◯◯◯◯◯◯◯◯ "

165

JUMBLE®

Unscramble these six Jumbles, one letter to each square, to form six ordinary words.

RIELOO

ZERBAN

NAGUMM

AXROTH

JUNIER

EECCAD

DOG-CATCHER

WHAT THE POOCH WHO DID NOT LIKE THE IDEA OF DOG POUNDS DECIDED TO DO.

Now arrange the circled letters to form the surprise answer, as suggested by the above cartoon.

Print answer here

JUMBLE®

Unscramble these six Jumbles, one letter
to each square, to form six ordinary words.

TARRMY

YURGAS

REPJUM

SHUCOR

CHYPIS

TOPITE

WHAT A SUCCESSFUL
BOXER HAS TO
CONSIDER.

Now arrange the circled letters
to form the surprise answer, as
suggested by the above cartoon.

Print answer here

THE " ⬡⬡⬡⬡⬡⬡ " OF ⬡⬡⬡⬡⬡⬡⬡

167

JUMBLE®

Unscramble these six Jumbles, one letter to each square, to form six ordinary words.

FOUTTI

CRESPO

DEGAAM

NAUMUT

QUIDIL

REFILP

A ROAD MAP TELLS
YOU EVERYTHING
YOU NEED TO KNOW
EXCEPT HOW TO
DO THIS.

Now arrange the circled letters to form the surprise answer, as suggested by the above cartoon.

Print answer here

JUMBLE®

Unscramble these six Jumbles, one letter
to each square, to form six ordinary words.

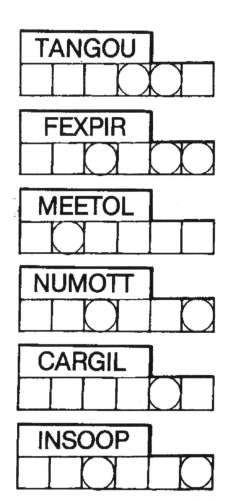

TANGOU

FEXPIR

MEETOL

NUMOTT

CARGIL

INSOOP

A POLITICIAN USUALLY STANDS ON HIS RECORD IN ORDER TO KEEP THE VOTERS FROM DOING THIS.

Now arrange the circled letters
to form the surprise answer, as
suggested by the above cartoon.

Print answer here

JUMBLE®

Unscramble these six Jumbles, one letter
to each square, to form six ordinary words.

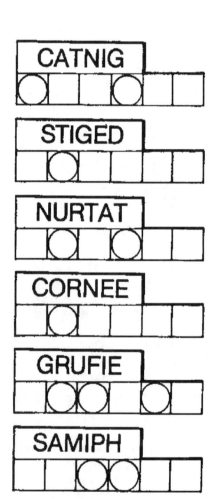

CATNIG

STIGED

NURTAT

CORNEE

GRUFIE

SAMIPH

What's he doing
here, anyway?

THE KIND OF
STORY A
BALD MAN MIGHT
LIKE TO HEAR.

Now arrange the circled letters
to form the surprise answer, as
suggested by the above cartoon.

Print answer here

A ⬡⬡⬡⬡ - ⬡⬡⬡⬡⬡⬡⬡⬡ ONE

JUMBLE

Unscramble these six Jumbles, one letter to each square, to form six ordinary words.

SLAVIE

YARPTS

LAAXYG

FRIMAF

TIMCAP

RYNFEZ

Walking was the quickest way to get here

AJAX EMPLOYMENT AGENCY

HOW TO GET AHEAD IN THE BIG CITY.

Now arrange the circled letters to form the surprise answer, as suggested by the above cartoon.

Print answer here

OUT OF

JUMBLE®

Unscramble these six Jumbles, one letter to each square, to form six ordinary words.

RUTOPO

SOOPEP

PURTET

RALMEV

YONCOV

HAILEW

We've upgraded our panels. Let me know if you need more energy.

We're good, you've really outdone yourself!

WHEN HIS NEIGHBOR INSTALLED TWICE AS MANY SOLAR PANELS ON HIS ROOF, HE SAID———

Now arrange the circled letters to form the surprise answer, as suggested by the above cartoon.

Print answer here

JUMBLE®

Unscramble these six Jumbles, one letter to each square, to form six ordinary words.

COLLEA

RUIJYN

RAWNOD

GUHONE

BBOSAR

TANEYL

AFTER FALLING SEVERAL TIMES IN A ROW, THE TIGHTROPE WALKER WAS NERVOUS. HIS ---

Now arrange the circled letters to form the surprise answer, as suggested by the above cartoon.

Print answer here

JUMBLE®

Unscramble these six Jumbles, one letter to each square, to form six ordinary words.

KRAMBE

UGATIR

NOLYEP

RICINO

MOSNMU

CCTIHE

Henrietta, you don't lay eggs like you used to. But we're both getting older.

I think it's time to retire.

THE HEN HAD LAID EGGS FOR YEARS. SHE WAS FINALLY READY TO RETIRE BECAUSE SHE WAS ---

Now arrange the circled letters to form the surprise answer, as suggested by the above cartoon.

Print answer here

174

JUMBLE®

Unscramble these six Jumbles, one letter to each square, to form six ordinary words.

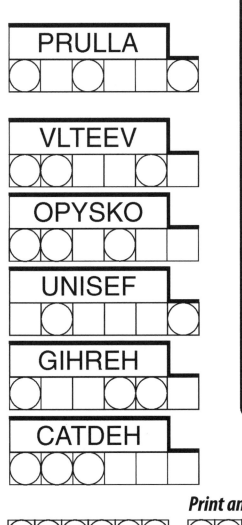

PRULLA

VLTEEV

OPYSKO

UNISEF

GIHREH

CATDEH

The computer sorts the mail, picks the street and the GPS aims the postal cannon. It delivers five times faster!

This is revolutionary, but I don't think the main office will approve.

WHEN THE INNOVATIVE MAIL CARRIER BUILT HIS OWN MAIL CART, HE ---

Now arrange the circled letters to form the surprise answer, as suggested by the above cartoon.

Print answer here

JUMBLE®

Unscramble these six Jumbles, one letter to each square, to form six ordinary words.

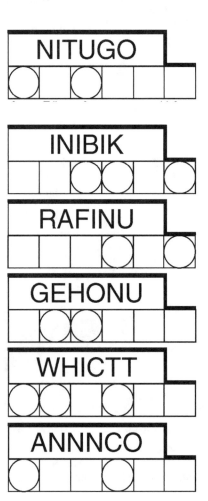

NITUGO

INIBIK

RAFINU

GEHONU

WHICTT

ANNNCO

No one is going to catch him.

One more lap and he's the champ!

WITH SUCH A BIG LEAD GOING INTO THE FINAL LAP AT THE INDY 500, HE WAS ----

Now arrange the circled letters to form the surprise answer, as suggested by the above cartoon.

Print answer here

JUMBLE®

Unscramble these six Jumbles, one letter to each square, to form six ordinary words.

CTILEK

THAMFO

RUHOLY

PIMAHS

MOCENI

SHAMAT

Where will you put it all?

I'm going to need one of everything. I also have food coming from another place.

It's him!

THE FOOD CRITIC WAS BEHIND IN HIS RESTAURANT REVIEWS BECAUSE HE HAD ---

Now arrange the circled letters to form the surprise answer, as suggested by the above cartoon.

Print answer here

JUMBLE®

Unscramble these six Jumbles, one letter to each square, to form six ordinary words.

BOGLIE

RANDOG

MYLHAN

LABELT

SUCACE

AAANNB

I can get you both of these parts for only 70 million credits.

That's what I paid for him. Do you have anything less expensive?

THE REPLACEMENT PARTS FOR THE ANDROID ----

Now arrange the circled letters to form the surprise answer, as suggested by the above cartoon.

Print answer here

☐☐☐☐ ☐☐ ☐☐☐ ☐☐☐ ☐ ☐☐☐

JUMBLE®

Unscramble these six Jumbles, one letter
to each square, to form six ordinary words.

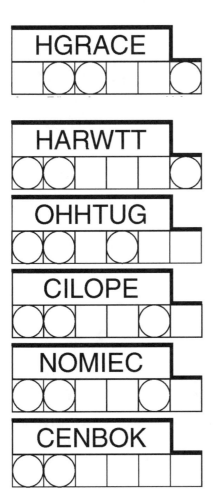

HGRACE

HARWTT

OHHTUG

CILOPE

NOMIEC

CENBOK

Wow!
He wasn't
supposed to
last one round.
That was fast!

Here's the new
champ with a TKO
in the first round!

THE BOXER WAS EXPECTED
TO WIN EASILY, BUT HIS
OPPONENT ---

Now arrange the circled letters
to form the surprise answer, as
suggested by the above cartoon.

Print answer here

179

JUMBLE®

Unscramble these six Jumbles, one letter
to each square, to form six ordinary words.

TARREH

SLAWEE

BUYEAT

TOOLIN

DYIRHB

THALEW

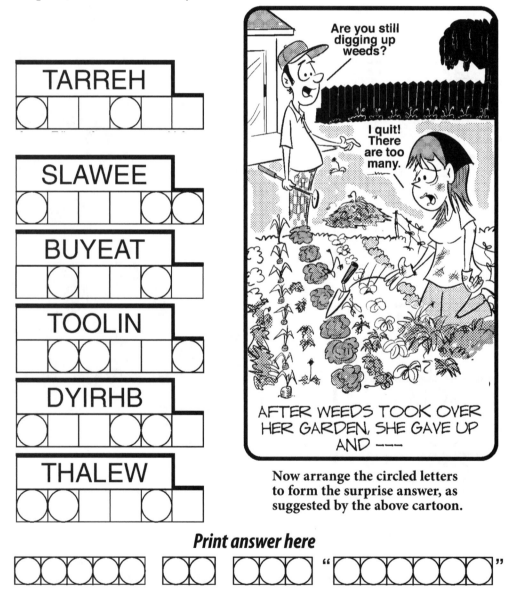

Are you still
digging up
weeds?

I quit!
There
are too
many.

AFTER WEEDS TOOK OVER
HER GARDEN, SHE GAVE UP
AND ---

Now arrange the circled letters
to form the surprise answer, as
suggested by the above cartoon.

Print answer here

◯◯◯◯◯ ◯◯ ◯◯◯ "◯◯◯◯◯◯"

Unscramble these six Jumbles, one letter
to each square, to form six ordinary words.

PARTUB

XREEIP

THIGCL

TONGET

GELUNF

DOHSAW

I can't believe you never let me hang out with my best friend.

I can't believe you wouldn't come with me to my family reunion.

THE ARCHAEOLOGISTS
ONCE DATED AND
COULDN'T HELP ---

Now arrange the circled letters
to form the surprise answer, as
suggested by the above cartoon.

Print answer here

181

JUMBLE®

Unscramble these six Jumbles, one letter to each square, to form six ordinary words.

CCINIO

OCYNTO

RUYGEN

HOUTAR

TOCXIE

SUNEGI

There he goes.

Yep! How can he jog while having conference calls and checking emails?

I'll have to call you back!

HE FELL OFF THE TREADMILL BECAUSE HE WASN'T ---

Now arrange the circled letters to form the surprise answer, as suggested by the above cartoon.

Print answer here

JUMBLE®

Unscramble these six Jumbles, one letter to each square, to form six ordinary words.

SBIYUL

FLEENN

ICANTT

ANDDIC

SLEUUF

SUEERF

Here baby, there mama
Everywhere daddy daddy
Hair, hair, hair, hair, hair, hair, hair
Flow it, show it...

It used to be great. But they looked bored.

I can see why this is closing night.

THE PLAY CLOSED BECAUSE IT HAD ----

Now arrange the circled letters to form the surprise answer, as suggested by the above cartoon.

Print answer here

" ◯◯◯◯◯ " ◯◯◯◯◯◯ ◯◯◯◯

Answers

1. **Jumbles:** VOUCH IDIOM BRAZEN GROTTO
Answer: How did the trumpet player manage to get into that exclusive party?—HE "HORNED" IN

2. **Jumbles:** JUROR SIXTY KINGLY COOPER
Answer: What you're likely to take when you're invited to dinner by witches—POTLUCK

3. **Jumbles:** TITLE RIGOR GIMLET WINNOW
Answer: What happened to the bell that fell into the water?—IT WAS "RINGING" WET

4. **Jumbles:** AISLE NAÏVE SUBDUE PUTRID
Answer: Why is venison so expensive?—IT'S "DEER"

5. **Jumbles:** BLANK TRACT MARAUD LEGUME
Answer: What happened to the plastic surgeon who was working in an overheated operating room?—HE MELTED

6. **Jumbles:** BROOD WHILE POORLY RADIUM
Answer: What's a parrot?—A WORDY BIRDIE

7. **Jumbles:** OZONE LLAMA PUNDIT QUEASY
Answer: Loves skin diving—A MOSQUITO

8. **Jumbles:** WHOSE CHEEK LIZARD SIZZLE
Answer: What his rich uncle who was a famous artist knew how to draw best—HIS WILL

9. **Jumbles:** LADLE DUSKY LOCALE CAMPUS
Answer: How the weighing machine tycoon started in business—ON A SMALL SCALE

10. **Jumbles:** MURKY OBESE UNCURL TYPIST
Answer: How to get your wife to bake those delicious rolls—BUTTER HER UP

11. **Jumbles:** DINER JUICY AMPERE FINITE
Answer: What the frightened rock was—"PETRIFIED"

12. **Jumbles:** DUCAT SOUSE CRAFTY KNOTTY
Answer: What to do when a plug doesn't fit—"SOCKET" (sock it)

13. **Jumbles:** LILAC GIANT TAWDRY NUANCE
Answer: What they were doing on that televised ballet—DANCING ON AIR

14. **Jumbles:** NIECE VIXEN LIMBER BENIGN
Answer: How the vampire loved—IN "VEIN"

15. **Jumbles:** SCARF JEWEL WIZARD BUCKET
Answer: If a hungry shark is in the neighborhood, feed him this—JAWBREAKERS

16. **Jumbles:** OLDER FRANC YEARLY NAUSEA
Answer: What the umbrella merchant was saving his money for—A SUNNY DAY

17. **Jumbles:** BUMPY ACRID COBALT IODINE
Answer: How does Jack Frost get to work?—BY "ICICLE"

18. **Jumbles:** DRAWL COACH WHALER MUSKET
Answer: The ship docked near the barbershop because they all needed this—"CREW" CUTS

19. **Jumbles:** LIGHT HUSKY DECODE IRONIC
Answer: The turkey crossed the road to prove this—HE WASN'T "CHICKEN"

20. **Jumbles:** AWOKE RUMMY CACTUS PICKET
Answer: What the railroad men said to the hobo who was trying to steal a ride—MAKE TRACKS!

21. **Jumbles:** OUTDO CLEFT DREDGE HARBOR
Answer: What the secret agent was complaining of—A "CODE" IN THE HEAD

22. **Jumbles:** NOOSE DOWNY BAUBLE TYRANT
Answer: Why they had to put the vampire away—HE WENT BATS

23. **Jumbles:** BLOOM FENCE MUSLIN LIQUID
Answer: What the doctor said when the patient complained of ringing in his ears—YOU'RE SOUND AS A BELL

24. **Jumbles:** IDIOT DOUSE JAGGED NUMBER
Answer: Why he quit working at the undertaker's—IT WAS A DEAD-END JOB

25. **Jumbles:** DOILY BRAVO STICKY FOMENT
Answer: When a vandal made a hole in the fence at the nudist camp, the cops said they'd do this—LOOK INTO IT

26. **Jumbles:** RAPID CRAWL ICEBOX LARYNX
Answer: What he got when he read the story about those body snatchers—CARRIED AWAY

27. **Jumbles:** PHOTO SQUAB LEAVEN IMPUGN
Answer: What "HMS Pinafore" could undoubtedly be—"NAME FOR SHIP"

28. **Jumbles:** KNEEL PROBE VORTEX LEGACY
Answer: What you might expect a pool-playing thief to do—POCKET THE BALL

29. **Jumbles:** PAYEE WAFER BLITHE QUAVER
Answer: Why she dived into the sea—TO GET A WAVE IN HER HAIR

30. **Jumbles:** JADED EVOKE NEARBY ELICIT
Answer: One cat told the other to be careful lest he do this—END UP IN THAT RACKET

31. **Jumbles:** LANKY ORBIT CASKET ALPACA
Answer: What chiropractors can expect a lot of—BACK TALK

32. **Jumbles:** GLOVE DROOP JAUNTY HOMING
Answer: He decided to become an astronaut when his wife told him he was this—NO EARTHLY GOOD

33. **Jumbles:** NIPPY BASIN INTONE ADRIFT
Answer: If you want to start losing weight, you can get initiated from this—A "DIETITIAN"

34. **Jumbles:** PARCH FANCY ERMINE SURTAX
Answer: "Where do all the fleas go in the winter?"—"SEARCH ME"

35. **Jumbles:** GRIME FAINT GLOOMY DRUDGE
Answer: The coffee tycoon decided to retire because he couldn't stand this—THE DAILY "GRIND"

36. **Jumbles:** UNITY FOIST OPAQUE SPLICE
Answer: What a wisecracker does—FLIPS QUIPS

37. **Jumbles:** ITCHY COMET FIASCO SPORTY
Answer: What he said her new headgear was—A "HAT-ROCITY"

38. **Jumbles:** GROUP WHOOP VENDOR PLURAL
Answer: The tuba player liked his work because he was this—WRAPPED UP IN IT

39. **Jumbles:** POISE ADAPT EMBRYO DEFILE
Answer: How a stag is often forced to run—FOR "DEER" LIFE

40. **Jumbles:** RHYME BIRCH TREATY VERSUS
Answer: She has many a suitor but none do this—SUIT HER

41. **Jumbles:** STUNG DOWDY VERIFY FROSTY
Answer: What people who growl all day often feel at night—DOG-TIRED

42. **Jumbles:** EXULT TYING MAROON POLICE
Answer: How society girls start in—BY COMING "OUT"

43. **Jumbles:** BLOAT FABLE ENOUGH INDIGO
Answer: What position does a monster play on a hockey team?—"GHOULIE"

44. **Jumbles:** INKED GUARD FERVOR MURMUR
Answer: This is a stern necessity on a boat—A RUDDER

45. **Jumbles:** JUDGE CHUTE VIOLIN TIPTOE
Answer: What a secret agent has to know how to do in order to hold his job—HOLD HIS TONGUE

46. **Jumbles:** THYME CABLE POETRY VACANT
Answer: What flatfootedness is for a traffic cop—THE ARCH ENEMY

47. **Jumbles:** BURST INEPT DOOMED POMADE
Answer: What a fall guy is—A DUPE THAT'S A DOPE

48. **Jumbles:** SMOKY CRESS SAFARI MISUSE
Answer: That Don Juan thinks it's never amiss to do this—KISS A MISS

49. **Jumbles:** HURRY BRIBE GAMBOL THRUSH
Answer: Those days were less hustle and more this—BUSTLE

50. **Jumbles:** CAMEO BOUND RANCID OFFSET
Answer: Where thrift is the best virtue—IN AN ANCESTOR

51. **Jumbles:** WINCE TWICE LONGER INFAMY
Answer: His son complained about having to cut the grass. He wished he'd stop his—"MOW-NING"

52. **Jumbles:** WHEAT GUILT THORNY FLIMSY
Answer: Mimes don't speak during a performance…Of course that goes—WITHOUT SAYING

53. **Jumbles:** HAPPY LOGIC DAMAGE HOLLER
Answer: The bottles of soda were on sale for a—DOLLAR A POP

54. **Jumbles:** IGLOO GRIND JOSTLE DEFINE
Answer: She wasn't sure the new billboard would work, but sales increased, which was a—GOOD SIGN

55. **Jumbles:** CLASS DRINK MODEST WRENCH
Answer: Having been dealt a royal flush, she won—HANDS DOWN

56. **Jumbles:** EXILE WRECK MAGNUM ORNERY
Answer: After the collapse of the Yuan dynasty, many in China were—"WELCOME-MING"

57. **Jumbles:** CROSS TRACK MIDDLE PLACID
Answer: It was hard to pull a prank on the magician because he never—MISSED A TRICK

58. **Jumbles:** HITCH FLOSS PANTRY MEADOW
Answer: The rabbit was dirty after digging in the garden and needed to—HOP IN THE SHOWER

59. **Jumbles:** AWARE DRESS UNFOLD FUMING
Answer: After realizing that they'd received only bulls, the new dairy farm was an—"UDDER" FAILURE

60. **Jumbles:** LOUSY BONGO FIDDLE FLORAL
Answer: The 18-hole course would be laid out in a circle, making it perfect for—ROUNDS OF GOLF

61. **Jumbles:** FATTY ICING STUDIO BOUNCE
Answer: The shoe store went out of business because not enough people—SET FOOT IN IT

62. **Jumbles:** FENCE DINKY EXPORT FILING
Answer: When asked about how identical they were, the twins were identically—INDIFFERENT

63. **Jumbles:** DROOP DITCH AWAKEN BREEZY
Answer: After reaching Everest's summit, he felt that his mountain-climbing career—HAD PEAKED

64. **Jumbles:** GRIME HOUND POTPIE PLIGHT
Answer: She offered the plumber soup that was—PIPING HOT

65. **Jumbles:** TREND LUNGE NEGATE RARITY
Answer: In 1927, going to see "The Jazz Singer" in a theater was a—"REEL" TREAT

66. **Jumbles:** FRAME CIVIC SEASON QUAINT
Answer: The horned animals loved butting heads, even with the—RAMIFICATIONS

67. **Jumbles:** BLAZE RAINY SMOGGY SHOULD
Answer: When the mosquitos swarmed during their carriage ride, they rode a—HORSE AND "BUGGY"

68. **Jumbles:** MINUS SNOWY FLINCH PACKET
Answer: After escaping his "Underwater Cell," Houdini couldn't—CONTAIN HIMSELF

69. **Jumbles:** STUFF TRULY MATTER REJECT
Answer: To collect taxes, the pirate government started a—TREASURY

70. **Jumbles:** TEETH KIOSK THRIVE POTATO
Answer: The patient was told to lower his blood pressure, and he—TOOK IT TO HEART

71. **Jumbles:** JOINT CYNIC SPRUCE MUTTER
Answer: The rhyming sheriff specialized in—POETIC JUSTICE

72. **Jumbles:** HAIRY AGILE ISLAND SWITCH
Answer: She wanted him to go with her to an estate planner, and he did it—AGAINST HIS WILL

73. **Jumbles:** GAUZE RUMOR SPIRAL SWIVEL
Answer: When it came to being a lead singer, Diana Ross was—SUPREME

74. **Jumbles:** CHIVE LOUSY KITTEN GAGGLE
Answer: After a long day of showing off his new electric bulb, Thomas Edison was—OUT LIKE A LIGHT

75. **Jumbles:** HITCH MERGE SYRUPY ACCENT
Answer: The flock of birds was selling its roosts and hoped that other bird would—"PERCHES" THEM

76. **Jumbles:** CINCH MODEM GLOOMY KOSHER
Answer: George V ruled Britain from 1910 until he left for this in 1936—KINGDOM COME

77. **Jumbles:** AROSE DROOP SETTLE PAYOFF
Answer: He asked her to marry him, and she said, "Yes." Then he—PROPOSED A TOAST

78. **Jumbles:** YOUNG BEGAN HERBAL RIPPLE
Answer: The new restaurant in Budapest did well, thanks to all the—"HUNGARY" PEOPLE

79. **Jumbles:** ZESTY UNITY PIGEON DRAGON
Answer: After riding the unicycle for miles, the rider was—ONE TIRED GUY

80. **Jumbles:** FUSSY NEEDY WIZARD BEETLE
Answer: The people on the platform waving to the departing train were—"BYE-STANDERS"

81. **Jumbles:** NERVY AGILE STORMY SHRANK
Answer: The wrestler thought he would win the match, but he was—SORELY MISTAKEN

82. **Jumbles:** SWORN HOWDY SNAPPY BUNKER
Answer: In a race with another reindeer, Rudolph—WON BY A NOSE

83. **Jumbles:** PANIC CLERK VASTLY THROWN
Answer: The new national book club had—LOCAL CHAPTERS

84. **Jumbles:** KITTY CIVIC INDIGO MINNOW
Answer: When the coin-production facility was completed, it was in—MINT CONDITION

85. **Jumbles:** HYENA FAVOR NOTION TEMPER
Answer: Restaurants in Tokyo sell sushi to customers who—HAVE A YEN FOR IT

86. **Jumbles:** PIXEL COCOA STIGMA BUTANE
Answer: When one of the barnyard animals got out, the other animals blamed the—"ESCAPE GOAT"

87. **Jumbles:** PITCH BURRO MIGHTY INFANT
Answer: The pigs who put on the musical loved to—HAM IT UP

88. **Jumbles:** ENJOY AGILE TARTAR CASINO
Answer: If U.S. automobile owners collectively had a favorite flower, it would be the—"CAR-NATION"

89. **Jumbles:** GIVEN GLAND WINDOW HARDLY
Answer: The arm wrestler was about to win and had the match—WELL IN HAND

90. **Jumbles:** CHEER NOVEL STODGY DISOWN
Answer: The superhero was a star on her softball team and not a—ONE-HIT WONDER

91. **Jumbles:** APRON HOIST DIVERT ARCADE
Answer: He wanted to bring up the subject of a pay increase but was afraid to—RAISE THE TOPIC

92. **Jumbles:** OUNCE KNIFE DECODE GLITZY
Answer: He couldn't believe the young goat could talk. Then the young goat said—I KID YOU NOT

93. **Jumbles:** VOCAL RURAL FONDLY HAGGLE
Answer: When the farmer criticized his neighbor's corn crop, he got—AN EARFUL

94. **Jumbles:** SIGHT AMAZE LESSON BUCKET
Answer: As the cruise ship rocked, the struggling crew and passengers were—IN THE SAME BOAT

95. **Jumbles:** NAVAL GUESS DEVOUR KETTLE
Answer: The lemonade seller wanted her business to—STAND OUT

96. **Jumbles:** FLOOR SCARF NOBODY GOSSIP
Answer: When asked how her long-distance relationship was going, she said—SO FAR, SO GOOD

97. **Jumbles:** PERKY PATIO FAMILY UPDATE
Answer: When the gymnastics team won the competition, they—FLIPPED OUT

98. **Jumbles:** SWEET MOVIE SCULPT PARLOR
Answer: The jigsaw puzzles of the Mona Lisa, David and Venus de Milo were—MASTERPIECES

99. **Jumbles:** GECKO FLUID THRASH SHAKEN
Answer: After becoming a teacher in Sleepy Hollow, the horseman was—HEAD OF THE CLASS

100. **Jumbles:** TWINE FOGGY JOVIAL RAFFLE
Answer: The farmer took a photo of his wheat field with an old camera, but the photo was—GRAINY

101. **Jumbles:** GIANT BROKE SKINNY TIPTOE
Answer: He said he was going to win the poker tournament, but his wife wasn't—BETTING ON IT

102. **Jumbles:** PRONG WHILE PUPPET RADISH
Answer: The interview with undersea-explorer Jacques Cousteau was—IN-DEPTH

103. **Jumbles:** TOXIC HURRY BUSHEL FONDUE
Answer: Trying to putt with so many geese on the green was—FOR THE BIRDS

104. **Jumbles:** WOOZY BLOOM BUTTER WALNUT
Answer: Shakespeare couldn't remember the apartment number. Was it—"TWO-B," OR NOT "TWO-B"?

105. **Jumbles:** FORCE LANKY TUXEDO WHIMSY
Answer: Being at the bottom of most maps, you need to look down to see Antarctica's—"LOW-CATION"

106. **Jumbles:** EAGLE WHIRL AGENCY GLADLY
Answer: The vet that specialized in treating waterfowl had a—"WADING AREA"

107. **Jumbles:** ELDER TUNER CLAMOR LAWFUL
Answer: After winning new windows at the grand opening, they owned them—FREE AND CLEAR

108. **Jumbles:** CURLY TRUCK ADMIRE GALLON
Answer: The story about the diamond and its setting didn't—RING TRUE

109. **Jumbles:** SALAD TULIP SOCKET FOSSIL
Answer: The magazine's employees didn't work well together and had—A LOT OF ISSUES

110. **Jumbles:** AGAIN EXUDE CRAFTY PUNDIT
Answer: All the students at the school prom were in—"ATTEND-DANCE"

111. **Jumbles:** DWARF STOOD HONCHO CRUTCH
Answer: The seven and nine didn't get along and were often—AT ODDS

112. **Jumbles:** FINCH RURAL MIDDLE CAMERA
Answer: The head of the recliner factory was the—CHAIRMAN

113. **Jumbles:** PETTY HONOR FAMOUS CLAMLY
Answer: He didn't do so well on his algebra test and worried about the—AFTERMATH

114. **Jumbles:** KNIFE DOUBT LAGOON MISUSE
Answer: The skunks knew exactly when to spray, thanks to—GOOD "IN-STINKS"

115. **Jumbles:** FAULT PORCH HYBRID NEEDLE
Answer: Mount Rushmore's supervisor was needed, so he prepared to—HEAD UP THERE

116. **Jumbles:** HOUSE BROOK PETITE CACTUS
Answer: All eyes were on the actress as she ascended. She happily—TOOK THE "STARES"

117. **Jumbles:** ANNEX DIRTY LAPTOP MURMUR
Answer: When the giant animals argued over bamboo, the result was—"PANDA-MONIUM"

118. **Jumbles:** DAFFY WRECK REVERT BYPASS
Answer: She wanted to make an omelet quickly and had eggs that she needed to—BREAK FAST

119. **Jumbles:** STAND LARVA BURGER FIGURE
Answer: He was going to a black-tie event and needed an outfit that was—SUITABLE

120. **Jumbles:** NUDGE ABATE SCRIPT LATELY
Answer: The importance of the Wright brothers' success could be seen—"PLANE" AS DAY

121. **Jumbles:** SHOWN ADAPT DEFECT WETTER
Answer: The high-tech sculpture of Alaska was—STATE OF THE ART

122. **Jumbles:** ROBIN WHARF POETRY DELUGE
Answer: The Vikings were just about home after a long—"ROWED" TRIP

123. **Jumbles:** SOGGY DODGE PRANCE NUGGET
Answer: The installation of the city's new traffic light was—STOP-AND-GO

124. **Jumbles:** POUND SHYLY POLICE BREEZY
Answer: The helicopter pilot who became a chef was a—CHOPPER

125. **Jumbles:** FATTY DRESS PARADE ACTIVE
Answer: The couple once happily sailed together, but, over time, they—DRIFTED APART

126. **Jumbles:** ALLEY SEIZE WOBBLE VICTOR
Answer: When he gave her a heart-shaped sugar cookie, she thought it was—VERY SWEET

127. **Jumbles:** STUNG HALVE EMBARK GYPSUM
Answer: When B.B. King passed away in 2015, his fans—SANG THE BLUES

128. **Jumbles:** TITLE SLANT VASTLY AVENGE
Answer: They knew the time of the author's reading because of the—TELL-TALE SIGNS

129. **Jumbles:** WRING ELOPE TENANT BEHIND
Answer: To become successful, the musicians would—BAND TOGETHER

130. **Jumbles:** WHACK THYME EIGHTY SIDING
Answer: The app that could translate "hello" into any language was—"HI"-TECH

131. **Jumbles:** KOALA WOVEN TOWARD REDEYE
Answer: When teaching her kids about the Mariana Trench, she gave them the—LOWDOWN

132. **Jumbles:** LLAMA BOSSY LESSON TIPTOE
Answer: When asked if she could finish the dress in an hour, she said it—"SEAMS" POSSIBLE

133. **Jumbles:** MESSY DOUSE FLINCH EMBODY
Answer: The company couldn't make a profit selling origami, so the—BUSINESS FOLDED

134. **Jumbles:** OFFER ITCHY GENIUS NUANCE
Answer: The rhinoceros showed how rude he was by—HORNING IN

135. **Jumbles:** WAVER HAPPY KETTLE ACCESS
Answer: The background check on the cartoonist showed that he had a—SKETCHY PAST

136. **Jumbles:** DATED BLIMP LUXURY BLURRY
Answer: The weightlifter who dropped the weight on his foot was a—DUMBBELL

137. **Jumbles:** BLAND PRONG LIMBER ACCUSE
Answer: The four-star military commanders retired and became part of the—GENERAL PUBLIC

138. **Jumbles:** KNOCK STRUM ORIGIN BUFFET
Answer: When it came to music in the mid-1960s the Beatles were at the—"FOUR-FRONT"

139. **Jumbles:** TOKEN FACET FUTILE HARASS
Answer: The man who passed out when told he'd need bypass surgery was—FAINT OF HEART

140. **Jumbles:** BOGEY RELIC ONWARD CALLUS
Answer: To get enough firewood to warm up their home, he—BURNED CALORIES

141. **Jumbles:** FRAUD AGILE PIGLET BUNKER
Answer: The team was for sale for about $800 million. The price was a—BALLPARK FIGURE

142. **Jumbles:** THINK AFTER SMOOTH JUGGLE
Answer: He wasn't sure how much sandpaper he'd need, but he had a—ROUGH ESTIMATE

143. **Jumbles:** SWUNG HIKER SPRUCE PACIFY
Answer: After all the passengers left, the ocean liner was the—"CREW'S" SHIP

144. **Jumbles:** HATCH SHRUG STIGMA JUNIOR
Answer: After fighting over who made better breakfast, they would—HASH THINGS OUT

145. **Jumbles:** HOARD HOUND DRESSY MATURE
Answer: Competition between Mount Rushmore's presidents was—HEAD-TO-HEAD

146. **Jumbles:** TOKEN DRIFT CASHEW NOGGIN
Answer: The harbor master had a busy day scheduled, with several ships—ON THE "DOCK-IT"

147. **Jumbles:** NEWLY PLAID WEAKEN VISUAL
Answer: The winery's grapes were finally ready to pick. They described the taste as—DIVINE

148. **Jumbles:** ONION ROUND GATHER RUFFLE
Answer: As she tried out for the cheerleading squad, her friends were—ROOTING FOR HER

149. **Jumbles:** NOISY ROYAL GOATEE TARGET
Answer: The pizza parlor's employee found shredding so much cheese to be—GRATING

150. **Jumbles:** HARSH TRACT WAFFLE OPPOSE
Answer: During the big eclipse of 2017, the sun was the—STAR OF THE SHOW

151. **Jumbles:** ACUTE EXERT VORTEX PARODY
Answer: When the director asked the movie star to do the scene again, she—OVER REACTED

152. **Jumbles:** RAVEN ADMIT FOURTH COARSE
Answer: When the house painter called in sick, another painter—COVERED FOR HIM

153. **Jumbles:** FORGO EXILE ENOUGH SALUTE
Answer: The extra charge for the side salad at the golf course's restaurant was a—GREENS FEE

154. **Jumbles:** TEMPO GLORY VISION PARDON
Answer: The high jumper was successful in practice, but his coach worried he was—OVERDOING IT

155. **Jumbles:** PARKA FLUKE SCROLL UPDATE
Answer: The bird that accidently flew inside the house—CAUSED A FLAP

156. **Jumbles:** WACKY GLADE HUNGRY SHREWD
Answer: To get his tools where they needed to be, the auto mechanic had to—LUG WRENCHES

157. **Jumbles:** TASTY NOVEL THRIFT WEEKLY
Answer: The tennis player hadn't lost a single game to her opponent and was—ALL SET TO WIN

158. **Jumbles:** CRIMP MOOSE TARTAR BUSHEL
Answer: In early days of golf, the flags were made out of—"COURSE" MATERIAL

159. **Jumbles:** SUNNY RUMOR EMBLEM SHOULD
Answer: Hula Hoop sales were reported in—ROUND NUMBERS

160. **Jumbles:** TANGY ENACT RARITY OCCUPY
Answer: When the kitten scratched her arm, she suffered—"A-CUTE" PAIN

161. **Jumbles:** FASTEN ELDEST BUSHEL CLAUSE FERRET PITIED
Answer: The best weight-reducing diet is one that makes you do this—DESERT DESSERTS

162. **Jumbles:** INJECT JOVIAL FORAGE STANZA FORKED LIMBER
Answer: What they called the course for apprentice plumbers—BASIC "DRAINING"

163. **Jumbles:** ORIOLE BRAZEN MAGNUM THORAX INJURE ACCEDE
Answer: What the pooch who did not like the idea of dog pounds decided to do—GO ON A DIET

164. **Jumbles:** MARTYR SUGARY JUMPER CHORUS PHYSIC TIPTOE
Answer: What a successful boxer has to consider—THE "RIGHTS" OF OTHERS

165. **Jumbles:** OUTFIT CORPSE DAMAGE AUTUMN LIQUID PILFER
Answer: A road map tells you everything you need to know except how to do this—FOLD IT UP AGAIN

166. **Jumbles:** NOUGAT PREFIX OMELET MUTTON GARLIC POISON
Answer: A politician usually stands on his record in order to keep the voters from doing this—EXAMINING IT

167. **Jumbles:** ACTING DIGEST TRUANT ENCORE FIGURE MISHAP
Answer: The kind of story a bald man might like to hear—A HAIR-RAISING ONE

168. **Jumbles:** VALISE PASTRY GALAXY AFFIRM IMPACT FRENZY
Answer: How to get ahead in the big city—STAY OUT OF TRAFFIC

169. **Jumbles:** UPROOT PUTTER CONVOY OPPOSE MARVEL AWHILE
Answer: When his neighbor installed twice as many solar panels on his roof, he said—MORE POWER TO YOU

170. **Jumbles:** LOCALE ONWARD ABSORB INJURY ENOUGH NEATLY
Answer: After falling several times in a row, the tightrope walker was nervous. His—JOB WAS ON THE LINE

171. **Jumbles:** EMBARK OPENLY SUMMON GUITAR IRONIC HECTIC
Answer: The hen had laid eggs for years. She was finally ready to retire because she was—NO SPRING CHICKEN

172. **Jumbles:** PLURAL SPOOKY HIGHER VELVET INFUSE DETACH
Answer: When the innovative mail carrier built his own mail cart, he—PUSHED THE ENVELOPE

173. **Jumbles:** OUTING UNFAIR TWITCH BIKINI ENOUGH CANNON
Answer: With such a big lead going into the final lap at the Indy 500, he was—ON TRACK TO WIN IT

174. **Jumbles:** TICKLE HOURLY INCOME FATHOM MISHAP ASTHMA
Answer: The food critic was behind in his restaurant reviews because he had—TOO MUCH ON HIS PLATE

175. **Jumbles:** OBLIGE HYMNAL ACCUSE DRAGON BALLET BANANA
Answer: The replacement parts for the android—COST AN ARM AND A LEG

176. **Jumbles:** CHARGE THOUGH INCOME THWART POLICE BECKON
Answer: The boxer was expected to win easily, but his opponent—BEAT HIM TO THE PUNCH

177. **Jumbles:** RATHER BEAUTY HYBRID WEASEL LOTION WEALTH
Answer: After weeds took over her garden, she gave up and—THREW IN THE "TROWEL"

178. **Jumbles:** ABRUPT GLITCH ENGULF EXPIRE GOTTEN SHADOW
Answer: The archaeologists once dated and couldn't help—DIGGING UP THE PAST

179. **Jumbles:** ICONIC GURNEY EXOTIC TYCOON AUTHOR GENIUS
Answer: He fell off the treadmill because he wasn't—EXERCISING CAUTION

180. **Jumbles:** BUSILY INTACT USEFUL FENNEL CANDID REFUSE
Answer: The play closed because it had—"SCENE" BETTER DAYS

Need More Jumbles®?

Jumble® Books

More than 175 puzzles each!

Cowboy Jumble®
$9.95 • ISBN: 978-1-62937-355-3

Jammin' Jumble®
$9.95 • ISBN: 1-57243-844-4

Java Jumble®
$9.95 • ISBN: 978-1-60078-415-6

Jazzy Jumble®
$9.95 • ISBN: 978-1-57243-962-7

Jet Set Jumble®
$9.95 • ISBN: 978-1-60078-353-1

Joyful Jumble®
$9.95 • ISBN: 978-1-60078-079-0

Juke Joint Jumble®
$9.95 • ISBN: 978-1-60078-295-4

Jumble® Anniversary
$10.95 • ISBN: 987-1-62937-734-6

Jumble® at Work
$9.95 • ISBN: 1-57243-147-4

Jumble® Ballet
$10.95 • ISBN: 978-1-62937-616-5

Jumble® Birthday
$10.95 • ISBN: 978-1-62937-652-3

Jumble® Celebration
$9.95 • ISBN: 978-1-60078-134-6

Jumble® Champion
$10.95 • ISBN: 978-1-62937-870-1

Jumble® Circus
$9.95 • ISBN: 978-1-60078-739-3

Jumble® Cuisine
$10.95 • ISBN: 978-1-62937-735-3

Jumble® Drag Race
$9.95 • ISBN: 978-1-62937-483-3

Jumble® Ever After
$10.95 • ISBN: 978-1-62937-785-8

Jumble® Explorer
$9.95 • ISBN: 978-1-60078-854-3

Jumble® Explosion
$9.95 • ISBN: 978-1-60078-078-3

Jumble® Fever
$9.95 • ISBN: 1-57243-593-3

Jumble® Fiesta
$9.95 • ISBN: 1-57243-626-3

Jumble® Fun
$9.95 • ISBN: 1-57243-379-5

Jumble® Galaxy
$9.95 • ISBN: 978-1-60078-583-2

Jumble® Garden
$10.95 • ISBN: 978-1-62937-653-0

Jumble® Genius
$9.95 • ISBN: 1-57243-896-7

Jumble® Geography
$10.95 • ISBN: 978-1-62937-615-8

Jumble® Getaway
$9.95 • ISBN: 978-1-60078-547-4

Jumble® Gold
$9.95 • ISBN: 978-1-62937-354-6

Jumble® Grab Bag
$9.95 • ISBN: 1-57243-273-X

Jumble® Gymnastics
$9.95 • ISBN: 978-1-62937-306-5

Jumble® Jackpot
$9.95 • ISBN: 1-57243-897-5

Jumble® Jailbreak
$9.95 • ISBN: 978-1-62937-002-6

Jumble® Jambalaya
$9.95 • ISBN: 978-1-60078-294-7

Jumble® Jamboree
$9.95 • ISBN: 1-57243-696-4

Jumble® Jitterbug
$9.95 • ISBN: 978-1-60078-584-9

Jumble® Journey
$9.95 • ISBN: 978-1-62937-549-6

Jumble® Jubilation
$10.95 • ISBN: 978-1-62937-784-1

Jumble® Jubilee
$9.95 • ISBN: 1-57243-231-4

Jumble® Juggernaut
$9.95 • ISBN: 978-1-60078-026-4

Jumble® Junction
$9.95 • ISBN: 1-57243-380-9

Jumble® Jungle
$9.95 • ISBN: 978-1-57243-961-0

Jumble® Kingdom
$9.95 • ISBN: 978-1-62937-079-8

Jumble® Knockout
$9.95 • ISBN: 978-1-62937-078-1

Jumble® Madness
$9.95 • ISBN: 1-892049-24-4

Jumble® Magic
$9.95 • ISBN: 978-1-60078-795-9

Jumble® Marathon
$9.95 • ISBN: 978-1-60078-944-1

Jumble® Neighbor
$10.95 • ISBN: 978-1-62937-845-9

Jumble® Parachute
$10.95 • ISBN: 978-1-62937-548-9

Jumble® Safari
$9.95 • ISBN: 978-1-60078-675-4

Jumble® See & Search
$9.95 • ISBN: 1-57243-549-6

Jumble® See & Search 2
$9.95 • ISBN: 1-57243-734-0

Jumble® Sensation
$9.95 • ISBN: 978-1-60078-548-1

Jumble® Skyscraper
$10.95 • ISBN: 978-1-62937-844-2

Jumble® Surprise
$9.95 • ISBN: 978-1-62937-869-5

Jumble® Symphony
$9.95 • ISBN: 978-1-62937-131-3

Jumble® Theater
$9.95 • ISBN: 978-1-62937-484-03

Jumble® University
$9.95 • ISBN: 978-1-62937-001-9

Jumble® Unleashed
$10.95 • ISBN: 978-1-62937-844-2

Jumble® Vacation
$9.95 • ISBN: 978-1-60078-796-6

Jumble® Wedding
$9.95 • ISBN: 978-1-62937-307-2

Jumble® Workout
$9.95 • ISBN: 978-1-60078-943-4

Jumpin' Jumble®
$9.95 • ISBN: 978-1-60078-027-1

Lunar Jumble®
$9.95 • ISBN: 978-1-60078-853-6

Monster Jumble®
$9.95 • ISBN: 978-1-62937-213-6

Mystic Jumble®
$9.95 • ISBN: 978-1-62937-130-6

Outer Space Jumble®
$9.95 • ISBN: 978-1-60078-416-3

Rainy Day Jumble®
$9.95 • ISBN: 978-1-60078-352-4

Ready, Set, Jumble®
$9.95 • ISBN: 978-1-60078-133-0

Rock 'n' Roll Jumble®
$9.95 • ISBN: 978-1-60078-674-7

Royal Jumble®
$9.95 • ISBN: 978-1-60078-738-6

Sports Jumble®
$9.95 • ISBN: 1-57243-113-X

Summer Fun Jumble®
$9.95 • ISBN: 1-57243-114-8

Touchdown Jumble®
$9.95 • ISBN: 978-1-62937-212-9

Travel Jumble®
$9.95 • ISBN: 1-57243-198-9

TV Jumble®
$9.95 • ISBN: 1-57243-461-9

Oversize Jumble® Books

More than 500 puzzles each!

Generous Jumble®
$19.95 • ISBN: 1-57243-385-X

Giant Jumble®
$19.95 • ISBN: 1-57243-349-3

Gigantic Jumble®
$19.95 • ISBN: 1-57243-426-0

Jumbo Jumble®
$19.95 • ISBN: 1-57243-314-0

The Very Best of Jumble® BrainBusters
$19.95 • ISBN: 1-57243-845-2

Jumble® Crosswords™

More than 175 puzzles each!

More Jumble® Crosswords™
$9.95 • ISBN: 1-57243-386-8

Jumble® Crosswords™ Jackpot
$9.95 • ISBN: 1-57243-615-8

Jumble® Crosswords™ Jamboree
$9.95 • ISBN: 1-57243-787-1

Jumble® BrainBusters™

More than 175 puzzles each!

Jumble® BrainBusters™
$9.95 • ISBN: 1-892049-28-7

Jumble® BrainBusters™ II
$9.95 • ISBN: 1-57243-424-4

Jumble® BrainBusters™ III
$9.95 • ISBN: 1-57243-463-5

Jumble® BrainBusters™ IV
$9.95 • ISBN: 1-57243-489-9

Jumble® BrainBusters™ 5
$9.95 • ISBN: 1-57243-548-8

Jumble® BrainBusters™ Bonanza
$9.95 • ISBN: 1-57243-616-6

Boggle™ BrainBusters™
$9.95 • ISBN: 1-57243-592-5

Boggle™ BrainBusters™ 2
$9.95 • ISBN: 1-57243-788-X

Jumble® BrainBusters™ Junior
$9.95 • ISBN: 1-892049-29-5

Jumble® BrainBusters™ Junior II
$9.95 • ISBN: 1-57243-425-2

Fun in the Sun with Jumble® BrainBusters™
$9.95 • ISBN: 1-57243-733-2